ENGLISH - GREEK TRANSLATION

ACKNOWLEDGEMENT

I wish to acknowledge with thanks London Examinations and EDEXCEL for their kind permission to use some past examination papers in this book.

New Revised Edition

I.S.B.N.: 9780905313214

Copyright: Dr. Kypros Tofallis 1968 - 2014

Published and Distributed by The Greek Institute
29, ONSLOW GARDENS, LONDON N21 1DY

ENGLISH - GREEK TRANSLATION

for Beginners up to G.C.E. "A" level

New Revised Edition

KYPROS TOFALLIS, M.A., Ph.D.

DIRECTOR OF THE GREEK INSTITUTE
FORMERLY LECTURER IN MODERN GREEK STUDIES
NORTH LONDON COLLEGE AND UNIVERSITY OF NORTH LONDON

ENGLISH – GREEK TRANSLATION

CONTENTS

Introduction 5

Part One

1. Nouns and Adjectives – Singular and Plural 7
2. Possessive Pronouns 9
3. The Genitive Case 10
4. The Accusative Case 12
5. The Verb in the Present Tense – Active verbs 13
6. The Verb in the Present Tense – Passive verbs 15
7. The Future Tense 16
8. The Past Tense 18
9. The use of the Imperfect 20
10. Present Perfect and Past Perfect 21
11. Interrogative Adverbs 23
12. The Imperative 25
13. Comparative of Adjectives 26
14. General Exercises 29
15. Examination Papers 60

Part Two

16. Advanced passages for translation 66
17. Examination papers - GCE "A" level 109

INTRODUCTION

This new edition has been completely revised and new material has been added. I have attempted in this short work to serve a number of purposes. First of all there are hardly any books dealing with English-Greek Translation so this publication hopes to be of some help to all those preparing for examinations such as those of the G.C.E. 'A' and 'O' level and the examinations of the Greek Institute. Secondly I have divided the book into two parts. The first part deals with elementary passages leading to the examinations of the Preliminary and Intermediate Certificates of the Greek Institute and the G.C.E. 'O' level examination and the second part deals with more advanced passages which will be found useful by candidates preparing for the G.C.E. 'A' level in Modern Greek and the Advanced Certificate of the Greek Institute. The G.C.E. 'O' level is still examined in Greece and Cyprus.

In the first part of the book I have attempted to give some sentences and passages related to Greece and Cyprus. In the second part I provide passages of an advanced nature and on a variety of subjects, which will help the student preparing for advanced examinations.

Past examination papers from the various examining bodies are also used in order to enable the student to be aware of the standards required. Although for the passages in the early part simple translation is required students should, as they advance, be able to translate idiomatically wherever this is required. Although for the passages in the early part simple translation is required students should translate the meaning rather than word for word.

Needless to say, to be a good translator one has to be good in the language: and to be good in the language one has to read widely. One should read as much as possible and regularly, a newspaper, a magazine, the literature and the history of the country, for by reading widely one accumulates a rich vocabulary, one becomes acquainted with the syntax, the idioms, the customs, the traditions, the attitudes of the people and of the land that one is studying. One should also never part with a good dictionary and should refer to the dictionary at all times.

Finally, now that Greece and Cyprus are Members of the European Union there will be growing demand for Greek translators and interpreters. I hope that this short work will be a useful introduction to the subject and will be of some help to all those students who are working towards the GCE 'O' and 'A' level, or the examinations of the Greek Institute.

October 2014

Dr. KYPROS TOFALLIS

PART ONE

1 The Use of Nouns and Adjectives: Singular and Plural

When we translate from English into Greek it is important to remember that the gender of the adjective must agree with that of the noun. If the noun is in the plural, the adjective must also be in the plural.

Examples in the Singular

Masculine: Peter is tall = Ο Πέτρος είναι ψηλός.
Feminine: Mary is clever = Η Μαρία είναι έξυπνη.
Neuter: The car is red = Το αυτοκίνητο είναι κόκκινο.

Examples in the Plural

Masc. The Greeks are hospitable = Οι Έλληνες είναι φιλόξενοι.
Fem.   The chairs are white = Οι καρέκλες είναι άσπρες.
Neut. The houses are large = Τα σπίτια είναι μεγάλα.

1. John is Greek.
2. Helen is English.
3. The apple is red.
4. The pear is green.

5. The restaurant is Greek.
6. Nicos is a teacher.
7. Anna is a secretary.
8. Athens is a Greek city.
9. The coffee is not hot.
10. The newspaper is not Greek.
11. The apples are red.
12. The taverns are Greek.
13. The newspapers are English.
14. The doors are blue.
15. The Greek houses are white.
16. The banks are open.
17. The villages are small.
18. The kiosks are small.
19. The Museums are closed.
20. The hotels are expensive.

Notes

teacher = ο δάσκαλος, η δασκάλα
hot = ζεστός, -ή, -ό
expensive = ακριβός, -ή, -ό
pear = το αχλάδι
city = η πόλη
hotel = το ξενοδοχείο
hospitable = φιλόξενος, -η, -ο
museum = το μουσείο

bank = η τράπεζα
greengrocer = ο μανάβης
cheap = φτηνός, -ή, -ο
secretary = ο, η γραμματέας
newspaper = η εφημερίδα
village = το χωριό
grocer = ο μπακάλης
kiosk = το περίπτερο

2 The Use of Possessive Pronouns

Possessive Pronouns are formed with the adjective δικός, δική, δικό and with the Genitive of the Personal Pronouns μου, σου, του, της, μας, σας, τους. The first is used in emphatic statements. The second in unemphatic statements.

Examples of emphatic statements

This coffee is mine = Αυτός ο καφές είναι δικός μου.
This tie is mine = Αυτή η γραβάτα είναι δική μου.
This book is mine = Αυτό το βιβλίο είναι δικό μου.

Examples of Unemphatic statements

My coffee is hot = Ο καφές μου είναι ζεστός.
My tie is red = Η γραβάτα μου είναι κόκκινη.
My house is small = Το σπίτι μου είναι μικρό.

Note: Remember that the adjective must agree with the noun both in gender and in number.

1. My house is large.
2. Your garden is small.
3. Our trousers are expensive.
4. My shirt is white and my tie is blue.
5. Your shoes are black.
6. These shoes are mine.
7. These books are yours.
8. Their father is Greek.
9. Their mother is English.

10. Our shop is in the town.
11. This shop is mine (belongs to me).
12. Mary's house is in the village.
13. John's car is red.
14. Their friends are in the tavern.
15. Your coffee is on the table.
16. These soft drinks are ours.
17. These apples are yours.
18. My car is blue and your car is white.
19. Helen's friend is Greek and Peter's friend is English.
20. My house is in London and your house is in Athens.

Notes

town = η πόλη
skirt = η φούστα
soft drink = το αναψυκτικό
tie = η γραβάτα

trousers = το πανταλόνι
car = το αυτοκίνητο
shop = το κατάστημα
shirt = το πουκάμισο

3 The Genitive Case

The Genitive Case indicates dependence or possession. Notice the different article and the endings in the three genders.

Examples in the Singular

John's tie is red = Η γραβάτα του Γιάννη είναι κόκκινη.
Mary's dress is blue = Το φόρεμα της Μαρίας είναι γαλάζιο.
The hotel's brandy is expensive = Το κονιάκ του ξενοδοχείου είναι ακριβό.

Examples in the Plural

The books of the pupils = Τα βιβλία των μαθητών.
The dresses of the women = Τα φορέματα των γυναικών.
The eyes of the children = Τα μάτια των παιδιών.

1. Peter's shirt is white.
2. Helen's shoes are black.
3. Nicos' friend is Greek.
4. Andreas' books are on the table.
5. The tavern's wine is cheap.
6. Peter's friend is French.
7. The sea of Greece is blue.
8. The mountains of Greece are high.
9. The islands of Greece are nice.
10. George's father is Greek.
11. The children's toys are in the box.
12. Retsina is the wine of the Greeks.
13. The weather of Cyprus is hot.
14. The doors of the houses are blue.
15. Greece's sky is blue.
16. The watermelons of the greengrocers are cheap.
17. Anna's sister is a secretary.
18. The marks of the pupils are very good.
19. The salaries of the nurses are low.
20. My cousin's car is green.

Notes

island = το νησί
tavern = η ταβέρνα
cousin = ο ξάδελφος, η

high = ψηλός, -ή, -ό
toy = το παιχνίδι
mark = ο βαθμός

low = χαμηλός, -ή, -ό
sky = ο ουρανός
mountain = το βουνό
souvenir = το ενθύμιο
weather = ο καιρός

hot = ζεστός, -ή, -ό
box = το κουτί
salary = ο μισθός
nurse = η νοσοκόμα

4 The Accusative Case

The Accusative Case is used to tell us about the object. It is also used to respond to questions introduced by the Interrogative Pronoun **Whom** and **What**. Again notice the different article and the endings in the three genders.

Examples in the Singular

I love Socrates = Αγαπώ τον Σωκράτη.
I love Aphrodite = Αγαπώ την Αφροδίτη.
I read the book = Διαβάζω το βιβλίο.

Examples in the Plural

I help the tourists = Βοηθώ τους τουρίστες.
I help the women = Βοηθώ τις γυναίκες.
I help the children = Βοηθώ τα παιδιά.

1. I help Peter and Helen.
2. Nicos reads the Greek magazine.
3. Eleni helps her grandfather and her grandmother.
4. Petros sends the letter to his friend.
5. We buy our fruit from the greengrocer.
6. You buy your bread and cheese from your grocer.
7. Costas and Maria drink their coffee in the garden.

8. I drink my tea in the sitting room.
9. You eat your breakfast at eight o'clock.
10. Katerina eats her lunch in the dining room.
11. Yannis eats his supper in the restaurant.
12. Aristos goes to school everyday.
13. They go to the market every Saturday.
14. You buy fruit and vegetables from the market.
15. Mr. and Mrs. Achilleas buy flowers from the florist.
16. I buy bread from the bakery.
17. Marina buys cakes from the confectioner's.
18. I send cards to my friends.
19. Mr. and Mrs. Socrates send presents to their friends.
20. Andreas lives in Athens with his family.

Notes

magazine = το περιοδικό
grandmother = η γιαγιά
lunch = το γεύμα
supper = το δείπνο
butcher's = το κρεοπωλείο
confectionery = το ζαχαροπλαστείο
florist = το ανθοπωλείο
grandfather = ο παππούς

sitting room = το σαλόνι, το καθιστικό
dining room = η τραπεζαρία
vegetables = τα λαχανικά
bakery = το ψωμάδικο, ο φούρνος
market = η αγορά
Mr and Mrs = ο κύριος και η κυρία

5 The Verb in the Present Tense: Active Verbs

Active Verbs end in –ω and they conjugate in two ways: Verbs which do not take an accent on the last letter conjugate as follows: **-ω, -εις, -ει, -ουμε, -ετε, -ουν**. Verbs taking an accent on the last letter conjugate as follows: **-ώ, -άς, -ά, -ούμε (άμε), -άτε, -ούν**. There are some exceptions to the above rules.

So remember the above endings when translating.
1. George drinks lemonade in the cafe
2. Maria eats mousaka in the restaurant.
3. We eat in our dining room.
4. We stay at the Acropolis Hotel.
5. They go to the beach every Sunday.
6. You go to the church every Sunday.
7. They go to school from Monday to Friday.
8. Helen sings in the tavern.
9. We dance with our friends.
10. They read the Greek newspapers.
11. You send cards to your friends.
12. Yiannis goes to Rhodes every summer.
13. Katerina goes to Crete every spring.
14. They stay in Athens in winter.
15. We go to our villages in the autumn.
16. The Greeks help the tourists.
17. We celebrate Christmas in December.
18. We celebrate Easter in April.
19. Maria buys fruit from the greengrocer.
20. Nicholas buys many things from the grocer.
21. I wear a raincoat in winter.
22. The priest marries the couple.
23. I do not live in Athens, I live in Corinth.
24. Every night we watch television.
25. They go to the theatre in Epidavros.

Notes

cafe = το καφενείο
church = η εκκλησία
I dance = χορεύω

spring = η άνοιξη
winter = ο χειμώνας
easter = το Πάσχα, η Λαμπρή

raincoat = το παλτό
beach = η παραλία, πλαζ
priest = ο παπάς
couple = το ζευγάρι
watch = παρακολουθώ
hotel = το ξενοδοχείο
I sing = τραγουδώ

summer = το καλοκαίρι
autumn = το φθινόπωρο
celebrate = γιορτάζω
christmas = τα χριστούγεννα
island = το νησί
to marry = παντρεύω

6 The Verb in the Present Tense: Passive Verbs

Passive Verbs end in **–ομαι** or **–ιέμαι** or **–ούμαι**. These are conjugated as follows:

(a) –ομαι, -εσαι, -εται, -όμαστε, -εστε, -ονται
(b) –ιέμαι, -ιέσαι, -ιέται, -ιόμαστε, -ιέστε, -ιούνται
(c) –ούμαι, -άσαι, -άται, -ούμαστε, -άστε, -ούνται

1. I visit Greece every year
2. We visit Crete every summer.
3. We are learning Greek.
4. I am learning English and French.
5. They get married on Sunday.
6. You remember your friends.
7. They are examined by the doctor.
8. We are getting engaged in June.
9. They visit Athens every year.
10. George does not sleep during the day.
11. I get dressed at seven o'clock.
12. I get ready to go to work.
13. Maria is bored in the village.
14. Christina visits the museum.
15. I come to College every week.

16. We do not come to the same hotel.
17. She is kissed by her parents.
18. Marios sleeps from eleven until seven.
19. We remember our relatives.
20. Daphne is not learning French.
21. We are examined in Greek.
22. We are tourists and we love Greece.
23. They stand on the Acropolis.
24. Costas does not shave every morning.
25. They get ready to read.

Notes

I visit = επισκέπτομαι
to marry = παντρεύω (-ομαι)
I am kissed = φιλιέμαι
I sleep = κοιμάμαι (-ούμαι)
I am learning = διδάσκομαι
I remember = θυμάμαι (-ούμαι)
parents = οι γονείς
during = κατά τη διάρκεια

I get dressed = ντύνομαι
I am bored = βαριέμαι
I am examined = εξετάζομαι
I stand = στέκομαι
I get ready = ετοιμάζομαι
I come = έρχομαι
relations = οι συγγενείς
I shave = ξυρίζομαι

7 The Use of the Future Tense

The Future Continuous is formed with **Θα** followed by the Present Indicative. Examples: I shall be writing = **Θα γράφω**, I shall be singing = **Θα τραγουδώ**. This is used when the future action is incomplete of repetitive.

The Future Simple is used when the future action is complete. Example: The shop will open tomorrow at eight = Το κατάστημα θα ανοίξει αύριο στις οκτώ.

The endings of the Future (both Active and Passive) are almost the same: **-ω, -εις, -ει, -ούμε, -έτε, -ουν.** The only difference is the ending of the 2nd person plural of the Passive which changes into **–είτε.**

1. We shall go to Athens in August.
2. You will go to the theatre.
3. They will visit the museum.
4. Peter will go to Thessaloniki.
5. Maria will stay with friends in Rhodes.
6. I shall buy many souvenirs from Greece.
7. Marina will stay in Crete for three weeks.
8. We shall eat in a Greek restaurant.
9. They will visit the Acropolis tomorrow.
10. We shall go to Olympia on Saturday.
11. Nikos and Mary will visit Delphi on Sunday.
12. You will see your friends in Cyprus.
13. We shall eat at nine o'clock tonight.
14. Andreas will eat his breakfast at eight o'clock.
15. We shall wake up at seven o'clock.
16. Christina and Markos will go to the cinema tonight.
17. You will come to College next week.
18. Elizabeth will learn Greek very soon.
19. I shall write to you from Greece.
20. We shall write to you in Greek.
21. They will not sleep tonight.
22. The family will travel by aeroplane.
23. The children will not travel by train.
24. The tourists will buy souvenirs.
25. The tourists will visit the sights.

Notes

museum = το Μουσείο
I stay = μένω
I travel = ταξιδεύω
soon = σύντομα
sights = τα αξιοθέατα
I buy = αγοράζω

tonight = απόψε
I return = επιστρέφω
I wake up = ξυπνώ
Delphi = οι Δελφοί
college = το κολέγιο

8 The Use of the Past Tense

Verbs in the Past Tense in the Active and Passive end in – **α**. These are conjugated as follows: **-α, -ες, -ε, -αμε, -ατε, -αν.**

Examples: I helped my father = Βοήθησα τον πατέρα μου.
I was taught Greek = Διδάχτηκα Ελληνικά.

1. I went to school on Monday.
2. We went to church on Sunday.
3. They went to the theatre on Tuesday.
4. They saw a Greek film.
5. My friends went to Crete.
6. The hotel was very clean.
7. We visited many places in Cyprus.
8. Marina travelled to Thessaloniki by train.
9. The pupils were in their classroom.
10. I was taught English in Athens.
11. We were taught Greek in London.
12. They went to the village.
13. Christos sent a letter to his grandmother.

14. Elli sent me a card from Cyprus.
15. We ate kebab and we drank retsina.
16. We danced Greek dances.
17. Aristos read the newspaper in the cafe.
18. I went to the sea-side with my friends.
19. The fields were green in the spring.
20. I bought many things from the islands.
21. Andreas sold his old car.
22. Elizabeth bought a new flat in Athens.
23. They stayed in Greece for three weeks.
24. Anna and Nicos visited many places.
25. We went to a Greek wedding on Sunday.

Notes

church = η εκκλησία
clean = καθαρός, -ή, -ό
pupil = ο μαθητής
kebab = το σουβλάκι
sea-side = η θάλασσα
I sell = πουλώ
Elizabeth = η Ελισάβετ
old = παλαιός, ά, ό

film = το φιλμ, η ταινία
place = ο τόπος
classroom = η τάξη
I dance = χορεύω (ο χορός)
field = το χωράφι
wedding = ο γάμος
flat = το διαμέρισμα

9 The Use of the Imperfect

The endings of the Imperfect (Active) are the same as those of the Past Tense, i.e. **-α, -ες, -ε, -αμε, -ατε, -αν.**

The endings of the Imperfect (Passive Verbs) are as follows: **-όμουν, -όσουν, -όταν, -όμαστε, -όσαστε, -όνταν.**

Examples:

I was going to school = πήγαινα στο σχολείο
I was visiting Athens = επισκεφτόμουν την Αθήνα

1. I was eating in the restaurant.
2. We were going to the Greek church.
3. They were drinking coffee at the cafe.
4. Despina was eating kebab with her friends.
5. Anna and Yiannis were dancing for half an hour.
6. The children were playing in the garden.
7. Old Nicholas was working in the field.
8. Helen was working in the hotel.
9. We were reading a novel by Kazantzakis.
10. The pupils were writing a story.
11. The tourists were walking near the Acropolis.
12. Demetris was selling newspapers and magazines.
13. We were celebrating Christmas with our relatives.
14. They were celebrating Easter in the village.
15. Nicos was drinking his tea and eating his biscuits.
16. You were drinking orangeade.
17. They were writing to their friends in Cyprus.
18. I was visiting my grandfather.
19. The children were watching television.

20. Aristos was playing football with his friends.
21. We were visiting Patra and Olympia.
22. Their friends were eating at nine o'clock.
23. Our parents were leaving on Saturday.
24. Athena was buying souvenirs from the kiosk.
25. We were admiring the Parthenon on the Acropolis.

Notes

half = μισός, -ή, -ό
I work = δουλεύω
football = το ποδόσφαιρο
magazine = το περιοδικό
kiosk = το περίπτερο
parents = οι γονείς

garden = ο κήπος
novel = το μυθιστόρημα
television = η τηλεόραση
I watch = παρακολουθώ, βλέπω
I admire = θαυμάζω
old Nicholas = ο γερο-Νικόλας

10 The Use of the Present Perfect and Past Perfect

The Present Perfect is formed by adding the auxiliary verb έχω in front of the 3rd person singular of the Indefinite. The verb έχω conjugates in the usual way, **έχω, έχεις, έχει, έχουμε, έχετε, έχουν**. Thus the right person must be used when translating.

The Past Perfect is similarly formed but using the past tense of the verb, i.e., **είχα**. This is conjugated in the usual way: **είχα, είχες, είχε, είχαμε, είχατε, είχαν**. Again, the right person must be used when translating.

Examples:

I have been to Greece = Έχω πάει στην Ελλάδα.
You have been to Cyprus = Έχεις πάει στην Κύπρο.

He has gone to Rhodes = Έχει πάει στη Ρόδο.
I had gone to Crete = Είχα πάει στην Κρήτη.
You had gone to Mykonos = Είχες πάει στη Μύκονο.

1. I have seen my friends.
2. We have been to the church.
3. I have seen this English film.
4. We have eaten mousaka and a Greek salad.
5. They have drunk two bottles of wine.
6. Maria has sung a Greek song.
7. Christina has celebrated her 21st birthday.
8. The Greeks have celebrated the "OXI Day".
9. Nicos has gone to see his parents.
10. The tourists have gone to see the Acropolis.
11. I had gone to the restaurant.
12. You had gone to the wedding.
13. George had gone to the cafe.
14. Helen had gone to visit her friends.
15. We had gone to Argos and Epidavros.
16. You had bought soft drinks.
17. Anna had bought a cheese pie.
18. John had bought a spinach pie.
19. They had seen a Greek play at Epidavros.
20. They had admired the view from the hill.
21. George and Helen had danced for twenty minutes.
22. They had stayed in the village for two days.
23. You had read a Greek novel.
24. Christina had read two Greek poems.
25. Vangelis and Despo had spoken for half an hour on the telephone.

Notes

bottle = το μπουκάλι
song = το τραγούδι
parents = οι γονείς
spinach pie = η σπανακόπιτα
view = η θέα
minute = το λεπτό
celebrate = γιορτάζω
admire = θαυμάζω
I sing = τραγουδώ

birthday = τα γενέθλια
cheese pie = η τυρόπιτα
play = το έργο
hill = ο λόφος
poem = το ποίημα
twenty-first = εικοστός πρώτος, η, ο
village = το χωριό

10 The Use of Interrogative Adverbs

These are words which are used at the beginning of the sentence and they introduce questions.

Who? = Ποιος; (M)
Who? = Ποια; (F)
When? = Πότε
Where? = Πού;
Which? = Ποιο; (N)
Whom? = Ποιον; Ποια;

How? = Πώς;
What? = Τι;
Why? = Γιατί;
By any chance? = Μήπως;
Whose? = Τίνος;
How Much? = Πόσο;

Note the words **πώς** and **πού** with an accent introduce a question. Without the accent they are conjunctions and mean "that".

1. Where is the National Museum?
2. Who is that in the car?
3. How did you travel?
4. What time did you arrive yesterday?

5. Who told you this story?
6. How much did you pay for the wine?
7. Whom did you see at the College?
8. Where did you go on Sunday?
9. Whose car is this?
10. What time does the aeroplane arrive?
11. What time does the coach leave (depart)?
12. How much does it cost to send this letter?
13. How much does the newspaper cost?
14. Which bus goes to the sea-side?
15. What have you seen in Athens?
16. Where is the cinema called Orfeas?
17. Where is the Estia Bookshop?
18. Whom did you send to the post office?
19. How do you get to work everyday?
20. When does your school close?
21. What time does the lesson finish?
22. How are you? How is your family?
23. Is your family in England or in Greece?
24. Where do you come from?
25. Whose bicycle is this?

Notes

national = εθνικός, -ή, -ό
I travel = ταξιδεύω
I tell = λέγω (είπα)
coach = το λεωφορείο, πούλμαν
bookshop = το βιβλιοπωλείο
post-office = το ταχυδρομείο

lady = η κυρία
I arrive = φτάνω
I pay = πληρώνω
I leave = φεύγω, αναχωρώ
bicycle = το ποδήλατο
I finish = τελειώνω

11 The Use of the Imperative

The Imperative is used in commands, demands or requests. The Imperative is formed by changing the final –ω of the Present into –ε for the singular (or informal) or into –ετε for the plural or formal expression. The same rule is followed to indicate a completed action by changing the final –ω of the Indefinite. The Imperative is also formed by placing the particle **Να** in front of the 2nd person singular or plural. Negative commands take **Μη(ν)** with the subjunctive.

For emphasis use **πρέπει** e.g. **Πρέπει να πάτε** = You must go. Negative: **Δεν πρέπει**, or **Μη πάτε** = Do not go.

Examples:

Στέλλω – στέλλε – στέλλετε (Present) = Send. (action incomplete)
Στείλω – στείλε – στείλετε (Complete action) = You send.
Μην στέλλεις κάρτες = Don't send cards.
Να μην στείλεις το γράμμα = You must not send the letter.

1. Send the letter to my friend in England.
2. Don't send him that book because he will not read it.
3. Telephone Maria tomorrow at ten o'clock.
4. Write to your grandfather about your success.
5. Read the lesson, please it is very interesting.
6. You must go to the Acropolis tomorrow.
7. Come to the theatre tonight, you can see an English play.
8. You must go to Epidavros to see a Greek play.
9. Eat mousaka and drink beer.

10. Bring me a coffee, please.
11. Get ready, the coach leaves at nine.
12. Bring me a bottle of ouzo, please.
13. Go to the airport, your friend arrives at two o'clock.
14. You must go to Crete, you must see Knossos.
15. Go to Cyprus, your friends wait for you.
16. Come to my house tonight, at eight o'clock.
17. Go to the shop and get some fruit.
18. Don't tell lies, to anyone.
19. Don't drink that water, is not fresh.
20. Don't eat that food, is no good.
21. Don't stay in that village, there is very little to see.
22. Go to the bank and change some money.
23. Don't change the pounds, change the dollars.
24. Don't drink beer, drink retsina or ouzo.

Notes

I get ready = ετοιμάζομαι
I wait = περιμένω
bank = η τράπεζα
I leave = φεύγω, αναχωρώ
I bring = φέρνω
play = το έργο

success = η επιτυχία
airport = το αεροδρόμιο
lie = το ψέμα
dollar = το δολάριο
I arrive = φτάνω
pound = λίρα

12 Comparison of Adjectives

There are three types (degrees) of Adjectives: Positive, Comparative and Superlative. To form the Comparative we change the ending of the adjective into **–ότερος (M) –ότερη (F) and –ότερο (N)**. The Superlative endings are **–ότατος,** -

ότατη, -ότατο. Or we may add the word πιο in front of the Positive. Adjectives ending in –υς change into –ύτερος, η, ο and –ύτατος, η, ο.

Examples:

ψηλός – ψηλότερος – ψηλότατος (πιο ψηλός) = tall (M)
μικρή – μικρότερη – μικρότατη (πιο μικρή) = small (F)
ωραίο – ωραιότερο – ωραιότατο (πιο ωραίο) = nice (N)

1. Costas is taller than John.
2. Maria is young but Helen is younger.
3. Brandy is more expensive than wine.
4. Apples are nice but peaches are nicer.
5. Crete is smaller than Cyprus.
6. Rhodes is a small island but Kos is even smaller.
7. George had higher marks than Costas.
8. Peter had lower marks than Andreas.
9. This hotel is more expensive.
10. The pine tree is the tallest tree in the garden.
11. The English weather is nice but Greek weather is nicer.
12. Greek beer is good but English beer is better.
13. French wines are better than Italian wines.
14. Andreas runs fast but Antonis runs faster.
15. Elena is the youngest girl in the class.
16. This coffee is more sweet.
17. The orangeade is colder than the lemonade.
18. The weather in Greece is hot but it is hotter in Egypt.
19. River Nile is longer than the River Thames.

20. Mount Everest is higher than Mount Olympos.
21. Watermelons are cheap in Greece but they are cheaper in Cyprus.
22. Clothes are expensive in Greece but they are more expensive in France.
23. This television is more expensive than that.
24. The B.M.W. car is cheaper than the Mercedes car.

Notes

tall = ψηλός, -ή, -ό
clever = έξυπνος, -η, -ο
peach = το ροδάκινο
pine tree = το πεύκο
fast = γρήγορα
hot = ζεστός, -ή, -ό
wine = το κρασί
high = μεγάλος, -η, -ο
expensive = ακριβός, -ή, -ό
watermelon = το καρπούζι
marks = οι βαθμοί
I run = τρέχω
young = μικρός, -ή (νέος, -α)

long = μακρύς, -ύτερος
brandy = το κονιάκ
lower = χαμηλός, -ή, -ό
sweet = γλυκός, -ιά, -ό
Egypt = η Αίγυπτος
cold = παγωμένος, η, ο
river = ο ποταμός
mountain = το βουνό
France = η Γαλλία
Egypt = η Αίγυπτος
Nile = ο Νείλος
Thames = ο Τάμεσης
cheap = φτηνός, -ή, -ό

GENERAL EXERCISES

14

In July I went to Greece. I like Greece very much. I arrived at Athens airport in the morning. I went to the hotel by taxi. The hotel is near the Acropolis hill. After lunch I walked to the Acropolis. There were many tourists from different countries. They all wanted to admire the Parthenon, I could see the whole city of Athens from the Acropolis. It was a wonderful view. I visited two museums in Athens.

One week later I went to a Greek island. The island was called Aegina. Aegina is not very far from Athens. I stayed in Aegina for three days then I returned to Athens. Athens is full of kiosks. They sell many things at a kiosk. I bought a few cards, stamps and some souvenirs for my family and friends.

Notes

I arrive = φτάνω
airport = το αεροδρόμιο
hill = ο λόφος
lunch = το γεύμα
different = διαφορετικός, -ή, -ό
view = η θέα
stamp = το γραμματόσημο

souvenir = το ενθύμιο, σουβενίρ
I walk = περπατώ
admire = θαυμάζω
I return = επιστρέφω
I sell = πουλώ
I buy = αγοράζω
thing = το πράγμα

15

I have many friends in Greece and Cyprus. Some of my friends live in Athens and some live in the Islands. I visit them every year. Last year I went to Cyprus. I liked Cyprus very much. The food was wonderful, especially the kebabs. The weather was very hot. The people are very friendly. One day I went to the mountains with my friends. We visited Kykko monastery on the mountains. There are many pine trees and the air is fresh. I also visited Paphos. Paphos is in the west of the Island. The Goddess Aphrodite was born there.

I like swimming and visiting places with an historic interest. There were many tourists in Cyprus. Most of them were from Europe.

Notes

I live = μένω, ζω
some (pl.) = μερικοί, -ές, -ά
kebabs = τα σουβλάκια
monastery = το μοναστήρι
pine tree = το πεύκο
goddess = η θεά
interest = το ενδιαφέρον
last year = πέρυσι
Europe = η Ευρώπη
most of them = οι περισσότεροι

especially = ιδιαίτερα
weather = ο καιρός
friendly = φιλικός, -ή, -ό
mountain = το βουνό
fresh = φρέσκος, καθαρός, -ή, -ό
west = δυτικός, -ή, -ό
I was born = γεννήθηκα
swimming = το κολύμπι
historic = ιστορικός, -ή, -ό

16

We have Greek neighbours. Their names are Petros and Maria. They have three children. They are very friendly people. We all live in North London. There are many Greek restaurants and shops in North London. Petros and his family go the Greek church on Sunday. Petros is a builder and his wife works in a dress factory. In the summer they go to Greece or

Cyprus and they stay there for four or five weeks. Sometimes they have a barbecue in their garden. They have many friends and relatives. The children speak excellent English but their parents speak very little English. When they come back from their holiday they always bring us some presents, usually a bottle of ouzo or a bottle of Cyprus brandy.

Notes

neighbour = ο γείτονας
north = βόρειος, -α, -ο
builder = ο χτίστης
dress factory = το εργοστάσιο φορεμάτων
barbecue = η σούβλα
usually = συνήθως
excellent = θαυμάσιος, -α, -ο
shop = το κατάστημα, το μαγαζί

family = η οικογένεια
church = η εκκλησία
I work = δουλεύω, εργάζομαι
relatives = οι συγγενείς
I comeback = επιστρέφω, γυρίζω
present = το δώρο
bottle = το μπουκάλι

17

Everyday I wake up at seven o'clock. I go to the bathroom and wash myself. Then I go downstairs to have breakfast. I usually have a toast, cheese and a boiled egg. I usually drink tea but sometimes I drink coffee. After breakfast I go to school. My school is not very far from our house and sometimes I walk there. I like languages and I am now learning French and Greek. Next year, I hope to go to University. I want to study languages. I like to travel to many countries. I think, you learn many things when you travel to other countries. When I finish school at four o'clock, I come home. First I have my tea, then,

I watch television for about one hour and then I go upstairs to do my school work.

Notes

I wake up = ξυπνώ
toast = η φρυγανιά
usually = συνήθως
I think = νομίζω, πιστεύω
I finish = τελειώνω
language = η γλώσσα
I learn = μαθαίνω
school work = η σχολική εργασία
I wash myself = πλένομαι
far = μακριά

I go downstairs = πάω κάτω (κατεβαίνω)
breakfast = το πρωϊνό, πρόγευμα
boiled egg = το βραστό αυγό
next year = τον επόμενο χρόνο (του χρόνου)
I hope = ελπίζω
university = το πανεπιστήμιο
I study = σπουδάζω, μελετώ

18

John is a young Greek. He works in a restaurant in Athens. He is married to Sophia and they have three children. Sophia works in an office.

John and Sophia come from a Greek island but they went to Athens for work. The family returns to the Island at Christmas and Easter. They always take presents with them for their parents. In the island they have a small field with some olive trees.

The children spend the summer holidays on the island with their grandparents. They go to the sea-side everyday. They also play with their friends. The children prefer living on the island because Athens is a large city with many cars, factories, smoke and noise.

Notes

young = νέος, -α, -ο
married = παντρεμένος, -η, -ο
I work = δουλεύω, εργάζομαι
field = το χωράφι
smoke = ο καπνός
noise = ο θόρυβος
grandparents = ο παππούς και η γιαγιά

I spend = περνώ (ξοδεύω)
factory = το εργοστάσιο
present = το δώρο
I prefer = προτιμώ
office = το γραφείο
work = η δουλειά, εργασία

19

Mrs. Socrates went to the shops, taking her young son Peter with her. They went by bus, Peter sat next to an old man with a green hat. When they reached the town, Mrs. Socrates and Peter got off the bus. The man was alone in the bus with the driver. They had come to the shops so that Mrs. Socrates could buy Peter a coat or some trousers. He chose a warm brown coat. Mother then took Peter to the park and bought him and ice-cream. "I don't want to go home before I've tried the swings," he said. They stayed at the park for twenty minutes. They saw the pond, the ducks, the pigeons and the flowers. Then they went to the bus stop to get the bus to return home.

Notes

shop = το κατάστημα
bus = το λεωφορείο
hat = το καπέλο
I get off = κατεβαίνω
driver = ο οδηγός
coat = το παλτό, πανωφόρι

swing = η κούνια
bus stop = η στάση
pond = η λιμνούλα (μικρή λίμνη)
duck = η πάπια
pigeon = το περιστέρι

I choose = διαλέγω   I try = δοκιμάζω
warm = ζεστός, -ή, -ό, θερμός, -ή, -ό

20

Greece is a small country. The population of Greece is about eleven million. There are many islands. Crete is in the south. Kerkyra is in the west. Chios and Samos are in the east. Thasos is in the north.

Thessaloniki and Pireas are two Greek cities. Both have ports. Many ships leave from these two ports. Many Greeks are fishermen. The White Tower is in Thessaloniki.

Ioannina is a town in Epirus. Patra and Sparta are towns in the Peloponnese. Kalamata is well known for its olives. Athens is the capital of Greece. Athens was named after Athena the ancient goddess.

Notes

country = η χώρα
million = το εκατομμύριο
south = νότιος, -α, -ο
west = δυτικός, -ή, -ό
ancient = αρχαίος, -α, -ο
population = ο πληθυσμός

north = βόρειος, -α, -ο
east = ανατολικός, -ή, -ό
port = το λιμάνι
god (goddess) = ο θεός, η θεά
tower = ο πύργος

21

Athens is a large city. There are many parks and squares. There is a University in Athens. There are many kiosks. The kiosks sell many things: newspapers, magazines, stamps, cards, sweets, ice-cream and soft-drinks.

The Acropolis is a hill in Athens. The Parthenon is on the Acropolis. There are many tourists there. Some people sell ice-cream and soft drinks.

There are many cars in Athens. There are also many museums. There is an airport near Athens. Many aeroplanes arrive from different countries. The airport is named after Eleftherios Venizelos.

Athens has a hot climate. In the summer, people sit outside to have their meals. There also many tavernas. The Greeks like music and dancing. The bouzouki is a musical instrument.

There are many newspapers in Greece. The Greeks start work early in the morning. Some of them do not work in the afternoon. In the summer, the shops and offices are closed in the afternoon for a few hours.

There are many villages in Greece. Some are small and others are large. Every village has a church. Greek customs are very nice. They have fairs in the villages. The Greeks celebrate Easter more than Christmas.

Notes

square = η πλατεία
kiosk = το περίπτερο
hill = ο λόφος
different = διαφορετικός, -ή, -ό
meal = το γεύμα, φαγητό

work = η δουλειά (δουλεύω)
custom = το έθιμο
university = το πανεπιστήμιο
matches = τα σπίρτα
soft drink = το αναψυκτικό

climate = το κλίμα   church = η εκκλησία
instrument = το όργανο   fair = το πανηγύρι

22

Cyprus is an island. The population of Cyprus is about 750,000. It is the third largest island in the Mediterranean Sea. It is very close to Turkey and Syria. Most of the people are Greeks (80%). Some are Turks (18%). There are some smaller nationalities (2%).

The goddess Aphrodite was born in Cyprus. She was born in Paphos. The ancient Cypriots believed in the same gods as the Greeks.

After the Trojan war some Greek heroes came to Cyprus. Tefkros built Salamis in the east of the Island. Agapenor built Paphos in the west. Praxandros built Kyrenia in the north.

Today, the capital of Cyprus is Nicosia. Cyprus was ruled by Britain from 1878 until 1960. Cyprus became independent in 1960. The first President of Cyprus was Archbishop Makarios. He died in 1977.

Cyprus has the following towns: Nicosia, Limassol, Famagusta, Larnaca, Kyrenia and Paphos. In 1974 Turkey invaded Cyprus. The northern parts of the island are under the Turks. Two hundred thousand Greeks lost their homes. They are now refugees in their own country. The great powers did not help Cyprus. Cyprus joined the European Union on 1st May 2004.

Notes

Mediterranean = η Μεσόγειος
close = κοντά
to be born = γεννήθηκα
I rule = κυβερνώ
archbishop = ο αρχιεπίσκοπος
I invade = εισβάλλω
power = η δύναμη
I join = γίνομαι μέλος, ενώνω
Trojan war = ο Τρωικός πόλεμος
most = οι περισσότεροι

I build = χτίζω, ιδρύω
president = ο πρόεδρος
I die = πεθαίνω
refugee = ο πρόσφυγας
help = βοηθώ
independent = ανεξάρτητος, -η, -ο
European Union = Ευρωπαϊκή Ένωση
nationality = η εθνικότητα

23

My dear Aunt Mary,

I have now been in Athens exactly a week. Your birthday present has helped to make this holiday possible. Our hotel is a very modest one, but central, being only a few minutes walk from Omonia Square.

This first week has been spent in taking Jane to all the places in Central Athens before we venture further afield next week. We have therefore ascended the Acropolis to see the Parthenon, strolled along Syntagma Square and later visited the Museum. Yesterday, the hottest day of a week we made our way up to Lycabetos Hill and gazed down on this beautiful city.

This coming week we plan to visit Sounio and Delphi (by coach), where Jane is very anxious to try out her new camera. I will write again later with some account of these excursions.

Notes

exactly = ακριβώς
birthday = τα γενέθλια
possible = πιθανός, -ή, -ό
modest = απλός, -ή, -ό
I venture = τολμώ (να πάω κάπου)
further afield = κάπου πιο μακριά
a few minutes walk = λίγα λεπτά με τα πόδια
central = κεντρικός, -ή, -ό
I ascend = ανεβαίνω

I strolled = έκανα μια βόλτα
I gaze = κοιτάζω
I plan = σκοπεύω, σχεδιάζω
I am anxious = ανυπομονώ, αγωνιώ
account = η αφήγηση, περιγραφή
excursion = η εκδρομή
this week has been spent = αυτή τη βδομάδα την περάσαμε (σπαταλήσαμε)

24

One summer evening, John returned home as usual at five minutes to seven precisely. When he opened the front gate he immediately noticed something strange. There was a heavy footprint and John thought it was that of the milkman or the postman. Then he noticed that one of the white curtains was open. John never left anything open.

He walked up to the front door and opened it quietly. He listened carefully for a few moments but could hear nothing. The front-room door was half-open. John wondered if he had forgotten to close it that morning. He had never forgotten before. Then he remembered that he gave the keys of the house to his brother because he expected some new furniture for the sitting room.

Notes

gate = η καγκελόπορτα (είσο-δος)
I notice = προσέχω
strange = παράξενος, -η, -ο
footprint = ίχνος, σημάδι
I expect = αναμένω, περιμένω
furniture = τα έπιπλα
carefully = προσεκτικά
precisely = ακριβώς
postman = ο ταχυδρόμος

moment = η στιγμή
I hear = ακούω
half-open = μισάνοιχτος, -η, -ο
I wonder = αναρωτιέμαι
I forget = ξεχνώ
sitting room = το καθιστικό, το λίβινγκ ρουμ
milkman = ο γαλατάς
key = το κλειδί

25

John: Hello, Joy. Back from your holidays? Did you go abroad again this year?

Joy: Yes, we did. We went camping. It was marvelous. We took the car across on the ferry to Spain, and stayed three weeks.

John: Not my sort of holiday, I'm afraid. I've never been one for camping. Too much like the army. Washing in cold water, and mosquito bites. No thank you.

Joy: Oh John, it's not like that any more! At least, not if you go to a proper camp-site. Nowadays it's not very different from being in a hotel. And much freer.

John: I'm still not very keen. I'm the sort of man who likes to have his meals cooked for him, and to sleep in a bed. And if we went camping, it wouldn't be much of a rest for Marion, either. She likes comfort as much as I do.

Notes

abroad = το εξωτερικό
this year = φέτος
camping site = η κατασκήνωση
marvelous = υπέροχος, -η, -ο
army = ο στρατός
mosquito = το κουνούπι
bite = το τσίμπημα, δάγκωμα
camping = το κάμπινγκ

nowadays = σήμερα, τώρα
comfort = η άνεση, τα κομφόρ
not my sort = δεν είναι του γούστου μου
any more = πλέον
at least = τουλάχιστο
free = ελεύθερος, -η, -ο
sort = το είδος

26

When Helen Keller was a baby, she was very ill and then became blind, deaf and dumb. She went to many hospitals, but no doctor or surgeon could cure her. It was thought then that anyone who was blind, deaf and dumb could never learn to talk or read and write.

Helen Keller was very clever and she did learn to talk, and to read and write. First, she learned to talk. Then she learned to read by touch. After a time she could write like other people. She wrote letters and books, and learned to read and play music. She traveled from America to countries all over the world.

Helen Keller loved life. She said life was an adventure. Most of all she loved children, animals and flowers. Many people who are not blind, deaf or dumb cannot do some of the things Helen Keller did.

Notes

baby = το μωρό   ill = άρρωστος, -η, -ο

blind = τυφλός, -ή, -ό
it was thought then = τότε ο κόσμος πίστευε
deaf and dumb = κωφάλαλος, -η, -ο
surgeon = ο χειρούργος
never = ποτέ
cure = θεραπεύω

it was thought = πιστευόταν
touch = η αφή, το άγγιγμα
adventure = η περιπέτεια
I became blind = τυφλώθηκα
I learn = μαθαίνω
most of all = πάνω απ' όλα
animal = το ζώο

27

William Shakespeare was a great playwright who lived in Stratford-upon-Avon and in London in the time of Queen Elizabeth I.

Most people say that William Shakespeare was the greatest playwright this country has ever had. Some say that he was the greatest playwright the world has ever known. His plays are known to people everywhere.

William Shakespeare lived in Stratford-upon-Avon as a boy and went to school there. In Stratford we can see the school he went to, and the house where he lived as a boy. It was in London that he wrote many of his greatest plays. Queen Elizabeth liked to see the plays he wrote.

After many years in London, he went back to end his days in Stratford-on-Avon. He was a rich man then and could live in a large house. We can see this house, which is near his school.

He was born in 1564 and he died in 1616.

Notes
William Shakespeare = Ουίλλιαμ Σαίξπηρ

Queen Elizabeth = η Βασίλισσα Ελισάβετ
playwright = ο δραματουργός
rich = πλούσιος, -α, -ο
in the time = την εποχή
to end his days = για τα γεράματά του

the world has ever known = που γνώρισε ο κόσμος
as a boy = όταν ήταν μικρός
known = γνωστός, -ή, -ό
play = το δράμα

28

In the days when Christopher Columbus lived, most people said that the world was flat. Christopher Columbus said that it was round, and today we know that it is round and not flat.

For some years he had made maps for a living and had learned all he could about ships and the sea. Columbus wanted to get ships of his own and sail them to the west and on round the world to the east. He learned of the journey to the east made by Marco Polo and his father, and how these travelers became rich in the east.

Columbus was not a rich man. He asked the king of Portugal for money to build some ships but he refused. Later the king and queen of Spain helped him to get three ships and the men to sail in them.

It was on Friday morning, August the third, in the year 1492 that Columbus was able to sail west across the Atlantic Ocean.

In October 1492 Columbus reached the West Indies.

Notes

Columbus = ο Κολόμβος

in the days = Την εποχή (τον καιρό)

round = στρογγυλός, -ή, -ό
for a living = για το ψωμί του
journey = το ταξίδι
I refuse = αρνούμαι
ocean = ο ωκεανός
I ask = ρωτώ, ζητώ
flat = ίσιος, επίπεδος

map = ο χάρτης
sail = πλέω, ταξιδεύω
traveler = ο ταξιδιώτης
across = κατά μήκος
I reach = φτάνω
Portugal = η Πορτογαλία
West Indies = οι Αντίλες

29

Joseph Lister was a famous English surgeon. He lived at a time when a great many people died in hospital after operations. Joseph Lister found out why.

Louis Pasteur had discovered that there were bacteria in the air and on things all around us.

Joseph Lister found that these germs could get into the blood, through a wound or cut, and poison it. He found a way to stop these germs getting into the blood. He used antiseptics – which killed the germs before they could get into the blood.

All surgeons in hospitals now use antiseptics. Nowadays people do not get blood poisoning after operations in hospitals.

There are antiseptics of one kind or another in most homes today.

Notes

surgeon = ο χειρούργος
operation = η εγχείριση
hospital = το νοσοκομείο
I discover = ανακαλύπτω

bacteria = τα βακτήρια
blood = το αίμα
cut = το κόψιμο
poisoning = η δηλητηρίαση

germs = τα μικρόβια
wound = η πληγή

antiseptic = το αντισηπτικό
kind = το είδος

30

Charles Dickens, one of the greatest story-tellers in the English or any other language, was born in Portsea in 1812. His father was a clerk and had very little money. When young Charles was only two years old the family moved to Chatham, and it was here that he lived until he was nine.

Chatham was a wonderful place for a young boy. Later, in one of his books, he described his surroundings as consisting of ' soldiers, sailors, Jews, and offices' .

In one of his books, 'David Copperfield', Dickens tells how little David, on his long, lonely walk from London to Dover, slept beside an old cannon.

When Dickens was nine the family moved to London. His father went to prison because he was in debt. His mother was poor. Charles at the age of ten was sent to work in a factory and was paid six shillings a week.

The visits which Charles paid to his father in prison and the unhappy time he spent in the factory were all remembered when he wrote 'David Copperfield'.

Notes

Charles Dickens = ο Κάρολος Ντίκενς

consist = περιέχω, αποτελείται από

language = η γλώσσα
story-teller = ο αφηγητής
clerk = ο υπάλληλος
I describe = περιγράφω
soldier = ο στρατιώτης
Jew = ο Εβραίος
cannon = το κανόνι
shilling = το σελίνι
were all remembered = τα είχε θυμηθεί όλα
David Copperfield = Δαβίδ Κόπερφηλτ

I move = μετακομίζω
surroundings = το περιβάλλον
sailor = ο ναύτης
lonely = μοναχικός, -ή, -ό
prison = η φυλακή
walk = η οδοιπορία
factory = το εργοστάσιο
unhappy = δυστυχισμένος, -η, -ο
debt = το χρέος
visit = η επίσκεψη

31

Paris is the fourth largest city in the world. Besides all the beautiful bridges and buildings there are magnificent streets (called 'avenues') which are wide and tree-lined. Perhaps the most well-known Avenue is the Champs Elysees, which leads up to the famous arch – the Arc de Triomphe (Triumph Arch).

Inside this Arc there is a lift to the top, so that you can enjoy more views of Paris. At the foot of the Arc is the 'Eternal Flame', which burns in memory of the dead soldiers of the two World Wars. At night the Arc is illuminated.

Almost every fourth shop along the Champs Elysees is a cafe or a restaurant. The citizens of Paris love to spend their evenings walking the avenues, or sitting at the cafe tables, watching the people of the world go by.

There are open-air cafes. The tables are set out on the pavement. Visitors to France enjoy this pleasant way of having a cup of coffee or an ice-cream. Like the French people, they enjoy sitting and watching other people passing by.

Notes

besides = εκτός
magnificent = υπέροχος, -η, -ο
tree-lined = δεντροφυτεμένος, -η, -ο
Champs Elysees = τα Ηλύσια Πεδία
Arc de Triomphe = η Αψίδα του Θριάμβου
top = η κορυφή
burn = καίω
illuminated = φωτισμένος, -η, -ο

pavement = το πεζοδρόμιο
bridge = η γέφυρα
avenue = η λεωφόρος
perhaps = ίσως
arch = η αψίδα
lift = ο ανελκυστήρας
eternal flame = η αιώνια φλόγα
almost = σχεδόν
memory = η μνήμη
open-air = υπαίθριος, -α, -ο
I enjoy = απολαμβάνω

32

This story begins just after Queen Victoria came to the throne. Jacob Marley had been dead for seven years. His partner, Ebenezer Scrooge, was the meanest man in London.

Scrooge was so mean he would not even pay for the paint to remove Marley's name from the office sign. It still read, 'Scrooge and Marley'.

It was a cold, foggy Christmas Eve, and a small boy with a red nose began singing a carol. Scrooge came out with a long wooden ruler, to hit the boy. Scrooge hated Christmas.

His heart was the coldest of all. At Christmas the temperature was freezing. He only had a tiny fire. His clerk could not fetch some coal without asking. His clerk's name was Bob Cratchit. He sat in a stool writing. His fingers were so cold he could hardly hold his pen.

People were going past in the foggy London streets. The air was smoky, so it was dark, even though it was only three o'clock in the afternoon.

Notes

throne = ο θρόνος
mean = ο τσιγκούνης
remove = αφαιρώ
foggy = ομιχλώδης
ruler = ο χάρακας
coal = το κάρβουνο
smoky = καπνώδης

partner = ο συνέταιρος
paint = η μπογιά
sign = η ταμπέλα
carols = τα κάλαντα
temperature = η θερμοκρασία
stool = το σκαμνί
hardly = με δυσκολία

33

At last the great day arrived. Cinderella began to cry. Her godmother, seeing her all in tears, asked what was the matter.

'If only I could... If only I could...' She was weeping so much that she could not go on.

Her godmother, who was a fairy, said to her: 'If only you could go to the ball, is that it?'

'Alas, yes,' said Cinderella with a sigh.

'Well,' said the godmother, 'be a good girl and I'll get you there.'

She took her into her room and said: 'Go into the garden and get me a pumpkin.'

Cinderella hurried out and cut the best she could find and took it to her godmother, but she could not understand how this pumpkin would get her to the ball. Her godmother hollowed it out and then tapped it with her wand and immediately it turned into a magnificent coach.

Notes

at last = επί τέλους
Cinderella = η Σταχτοπούτα
in tears = δακρυσμένη
wand = το ραβδί
fairy = η νεράιδα

ball = ο χορός
pumpkin = η κολοκύθα
hollow = βαθουλώνω
coach = η άμαξα

34

'Nasty day, isn't it?'

'Isn't it dreadful?'

'The rain... I hate rain...'

'I don't like it at all. Do you?'

'Fancy such a day in July. Rain in the morning, then a bit of sunshine, and then rain, rain, rain, all day long.'

'I remember exactly the same July day in 1936.'

'Yes, I remember too.'

'Or was it in 1928?'

'Yes, it was.'

Now look carefully at the last sentences of this conversation. It shows a very important rule: you must never disagree with anyone about the weather.

Learn this conversation by heart. If you do not say anything else for the rest of your life, just repeat this conversation, you still have a fair chance of being accepted as a highly intelligent person.

Notes

nasty = άσχημος, -η, -ο
dreadful = τρομερός, φοβερός
fancy = φαντάσου, σκέψου
rule = ο κανόνας

disagree = διαφωνώ
by heart = απ' έξω
accepted = αποδεκτός

35

In a small white house in the village up the mountain an old peasant and his wife told me their story. We sat at the table to drink coffee and the old man started.

'We came here, in 1935, because there was no work in our town. For a month we had almost nothing to eat and I worked twelve, thirteen, sometimes fourteen hours a day for very little money with which the whole family had to live. My wife will tell you what we ate!'

His wife put the cup on the table and moving her hands about she said, 'We had four children and we lived on bread and oil. Even the bread was so bad that we could hardly eat it. The soldiers laughed at us and called us 'donkeys'.

Her husband suddenly got up and continued with an angry face, 'I said to them one day, 'Give us more money, and we'll show you what we'll eat.' The army doctor laughed: 'You don't need any money. You don't understand money. You don't know what to do with it.'

Notes

peasant = χωρικός, αγρότης
donkey = το γαϊδούρι

suddenly = ξαφνικά
angry face = οργισμένο ύφος

36

When I came out of the shop, she was only a few paces ahead of me.

'Forgive me for speaking to you without knowing you,' I said as I went near her, 'but I'd like to know you.'

'Go away!' she said angrily and began to walk faster.

I couldn't think of any explanation for her abrupt manner of behaviour, except that I had perhaps been too polite. So I tried again.

'Leave me alone or I'll call the police!'

An old woman passing by heard her and gave me a nasty look. I stopped for a moment but then I hurried after her.

'If you keep on bothering me, I'll scream for help!' she shouted.

I gave up and watched her walk away. She looked back a couple of times to see whether I was following her; and the second time she turned around, she was laughing.

Slowly I walked to the nearest cafe where I met John. John was sure he understood women and told me that I was wrong to give up so soon.

Perhaps I was wrong but I still remember her beautiful laugh...

Notes

pace = το βήμα
angrily = θυμωμένα
explanation = εξήγηση
abrupt = απότομος, -η, -ο
I scream = ξεφωνίζω

behaviour = συμπεριφορά
polite = ευγενικός, -η, -ο
nasty look = κοιτάζω απειλητικά
bother = ενοχλώ

37

My mother's father, who lived in a village in Crete all his life, used to take his lantern every evening and go out in the streets to see if any stranger had arrived. Then he would take him to his house and give him food to eat and wine to drink. After that he sat on his bed, smiled and said to his guest.

'Talk!'

'Talk about what, Grandfather?'

'What you are, who you are, where you come from, what towns and villages you have seen – everything, tell me everything. Now, speak!'

And the guest would begin to talk while my grandfather sat calmly on his bed listening to the stories he was telling. And if grandfather liked the guest he would say:

'You shall stay tomorrow too. You are not going! You still have things to tell me.'

I have also found a guest and I will not let him go. He costs me far more than just one dinner, but he is worth it.

Every evening I wait for him after work, I make him sit opposite me and we eat. The time comes when he must pay, and I say to him:

'Talk!' I look at him and I listen. I never tire of listening to him. When he speaks, the whole of Greece spreads before my eyes with its mountains, its forests, its rivers, its men and women.

Notes

lantern = το φανάρι
stranger = άγνωστος, ξένος
I smile = χαμογελώ
I never tire = ποτέ δεν κουράζομαι

is worth it = το αξίζει
opposite = απέναντι
I spread = απλώνω

38

My friend Robert wanted very much to have an egg for breakfast. He took it and started breaking it carefully. It was hardly boiled and already quite cool. He called the woman who had brought it and he complained aloud. 'Please boil it a little longer,' he said.

We waited ten or fifteen minutes. The woman brought the egg back but the result was the same. However, determined to have his egg just as he wanted it, he called the woman again and trying not to show how cross he was, he said to her that he wanted his egg medium boiled. 'Boil it a little more – and quickly, please, I can't sit here all morning.' The woman said she was going to do her best, took the egg and left.

Again we waited, this time longer than before. I got up to look out of the window and I saw the woman walking across the square, with the egg in her hand.

'Here it comes' I said.

'Here comes what!' asked Robert.

'Your egg! She is holding it in her hand.'

'Where have you been all this time!' Robert asked when the woman brought the egg to the table.

'I had to take it to the baker's. Is it hard enough now?'

'It's just right,' he said as he was breaking it with his spoon.

He thanked her and when she left he said to me 'Now it's as hard as a rock!'

Notes

I complain = παραπονιέμαι
determined = αποφασισμένος, -η, -ο
to be crossed = θυμωμένος
hard as a rock = σφιχτό σαν πέτρα (σκληρό)
baker = ο ψωμάς
hard = σφιχτός
just right = κανονικό

39

Dear Anastasia,

Thank you very much for your letter. I am sorry I haven't written for so long but I have had a lot of homework. My exams are in three weeks time and I must pass them, so that I can go to university later on this year.

I am very glad you want to come to England for Christmas. It's the best time of the year for us and you will be able to meet the family and all my friends. I want to show you everything, all the sights, the exhibitions in the museums, the Tower of London, the Houses of Parliament, the zoo... It will also be a good opportunity for you to practise your English because I'm afraid that my friends do not speak much Greek.

How long do you think you will be able to stay? We have just moved to a lovely new house which is bigger than the one we had before, so we have plenty of room. It will be much cheaper than a hotel too! Perhaps you could cook us a traditional Greek meal while you are here! I am sure that it would make a nice change!

Write to me soon,
Lots of love,
Susan.

Notes

homework = σχολική εργασία
sights = τα αξιοθέατα
exhibition = η έκθεση
zoo = ο ζωολογικός κήπος

I practise = εξασκώ
I moved = μετακόμισα
traditional = παραδοσιακός

40

We live in a two-bedroom house, so as soon as my youngest son, James, starts calling 'Mummy, mummy', around seven every morning, he wakes everyone up. Being his mother I like to be the first to greet him, so I immediately jump out of bed to get dressed. I take him downstairs into the kitchen and start getting breakfast ready. Before long, the other kids are also down. If my husband, Paul, is working in his study, everybody tries not to disturb him. But if he isn't working, he gets up at the same time and has breakfast with the family. He often washes up, when everybody has finished and sometimes he comes with me when I drive the girls to school.

Because we live in the country, we don't go out much and most of our evenings are spent in front of the television. Anyway, after having worked in our garden, cleaned the house and cooked dinner for six, the only thing I want to do is go to bed and fall asleep reading my book.

Notes

I greet = χαιρετώ
kids = τα παιδιά
study = το γραφείο

to disturb = ενοχλώ
country = η εξοχή

41

Young people in Britain today find it very difficult to find a job. Joan Potter is eighteen and she lives in the North East of the country. She has been trying to find work for six months but she hasn't been very lucky. Her parents think she should go to university to study and become a teacher but Joan disagrees:

"My dad just doesn't understand. He thinks going to university will solve all my problems but I don't see it that way. I was never a good student at school so I don't think I should waste time and money by going to university. What I really want is to find myself a job and start earning some money at last! I buy the local paper everyday to look for work but haven't found anything yet. I would like to work in a big hotel or restaurant because I like meeting new people, but after all these months of trying I'll accept any offer. Some of my friends have moved to London, thinking it might be easier there, but they have all written back to say that they haven't been very lucky either. I'm so disappointed, I don't know what I'm going to do."

Notes

I disagree = διαφωνώ
I solve = λύω
local paper = τοπική εφημερίδα
I accept = δέχομαι

offer = η προσφορά
disappointed = απογοητευμένος, -η, -ο

42

Dear John,

It was very nice to see you last week. After you had gone I felt very sad. I still do. I really enjoyed seeing you again. I hope you enjoyed yourself too.

Two days ago I took my final exam, and it was pretty difficult. The papers are being marked now. My teacher told me that I would probably pass. I hope so! If I pass, I'll get a certificate. It'll be very useful... I'll be able to get a better job.

When you phoned, you said that you'd got a new job. Do you like it? If I were you, I wouldn't work too hard!

Last night we had a farewell party. We went to a new disco that was opened last month. The atmosphere was great! Everyone was in a good mood because they had finished the course. I'm going to miss all the new friends that I've made here.

I must stop writing now, John. I'm going to have my hair done this afternoon. I hope it won't be too expensive. See you next month. Will you be able to pick me up from the airport?

All my love,
Mary

Notes

I felt = αισθάνθηκα
I enjoyed = χάρηκα, απόλαυσα
probably = πιθανώς, ίσως
mood = η διάθεση

if I were you = αν ήμουν στη θέση σου
farewell party = αποχαιρετιστήριο πάρτι

43

John works two days a week in a London library – a job he shares with another two people – and spends the rest of the time at home. Pam, his wife, is a teacher at a local school and spends most of her free time preparing lessons or marking essays and exam papers. John looks after the children when Pam is at work, cooks the evening meal three times a week and they share the housework during holidays and at weekends.

John comes from a large Irish family and has three brothers and four sisters. "There was no question of not helping at home," he remembers. "We all did, including my father. By the time I was 12, I could cook for the family with help from my mother."

But doesn't he miss work? "Being at home with the children doesn't worry me at all, although sometimes I get a bit bored" he says. 'Right now, what I do is just more important to me than a successful business with an expensive car and a fast lifestyle."

Notes

library = η βιβλιοθήκη   I share = μοιράζομαι

weekend = το σαββατοκύριακο I miss = μου λείπει
I include = συμπεριλαμβάνω lifestyle = τρόπος ζωής

44

My sister, her husband and their two children live near a town called Horning. Ten years ago, it was a quiet country village I used to visit with my parents at week-ends, but now it has got much bigger! Every time I go there to see my nephews and nieces, which is not very often, there's always a change, a new building or shop, and sometimes I can hardly recognize the place! And there always seem to be more people in the streets!

Even now, however, there isn't very much to do in Horning, apart from taking walks around the lake or in the forest, but my favourite thing must be going into one of those traditional tea-shops and trying some of their delicious home-made cakes. The children love it too! We have recently discovered a new bakery, not far from the main shopping center, that sells fresh brown bread, biscuits, pies and lovely fruit-cakes. I always make sure that before I go back to London I buy enough to last me a few weeks.

Notes

nephew = ο ανεψιός walk = ο περίπατος
niece = η ανεψιά I discover = ανακαλύπτω
traditional = παραδοσιακός, -η, -ο

EXAMINATION PAPERS

45

She opened her eyes and saw David and Victoria sitting on the bed by her feet. They were looking at her with an expression of hope mixed with fear. She sighed and turned towards the window. She saw bright daylight coming through the curtains and murmured. "What time is it? I slept a long time".

Then David said, "Just a few hours. It was dawn when you closed your eyes. What a night! I will never forget it, no matter how long I live."

Memories of the events of the previous night came to her again and she felt sorry for the two friends who had sat up with her all night, sharing her pain and sadness. She moved her lips and whispered, almost embarrassed, "You both look so tired; it's my fault really."

She had barely finished her sentence when Victoria laughed loudly and answered, "It's true! We are exhausted but it is such a relief to see that you are better again. How could such a dreadful thing happen to you? Please, do not ever scare us like this again!"

David, shaking his head to show that he agreed with Victoria, said, "In any case, here's good news. This morning I told the doctor how you were doing when he phoned to ask about your health. He told me that the pain troubling you is a sign the broken bone is starting to mend."

London Examinations, GCE 'O' level, January 2000

46

How I ended up in the army, I am not sure. It may have been Jack's fault. It may have been my father's. It was the last day of school and the headmaster had stood in front of us for an hour, warning us about the future that lay ahead, outside the school gates. I had stopped listening to him after the first five minutes, and as I was desperately trying not to fall asleep, I noticed the poster on the wall about the army. Jack, who was sitting on my right, saw it too and whispered, "I wouldn't mind a few years as a soldier. Anything would be better than this! Think of all the exotic places we could get to see!"

I must say that, as I had absolutely no idea what I wanted to do with my life, the possibility of the army seemed quite attractive at the time. That same afternoon, we decided to go for the interview. We wore our grey trousers and our old school blazers but no ties. I think my father thought we were going to a party. "Have a good time," he shouted from within the kitchen, without even bothering to come to look. Even after we came back from the interview, having signed all the papers, I somehow "forgot" to tell him what I had done. Two months later, he still didn't know what I intended to do, nor did he seemed to mind. He never said "Get out of bed" or "Get a job", or "Do something with your life". He just let me decide.

London Examinations, GCE 'O' level, May 2000

47

The summer was almost over and it was late afternoon. It was Sunday. It had to be a Sunday, because that was the only time everybody was there in one place. Most people were kicking a ball around, a few were playing cards. The sun was unusually warm for that time of year, and everybody was trying to make the most of the weather. We had already been there for several hours but nobody seemed to want to leave yet, even though some of the younger kids were beginning to fall asleep in their mothers' arms. I was standing with Brian. We were sharing a joke when Lucy appeared from the trees, carrying a big basket of fruit.

'I've got some fruit,' she called. 'Enough for everyone'.

'Excuse me,' I said quietly to Brian, 'I'll be back in a moment.'

Lucy saw me as I ran towards her and seeing the serious expression on my face decided to speak first. She was going to lie in front of everyone, I realised. This made me even more determined! I stopped a metre away from her and stared at her.

'Yes,' she said loudly and slightly aggressively, holding up the fruit for all to see, and still watching me from the corner of her eye. 'Here is some fruit that I found.'

London Examinations, GCE 'O' level, January 2001

48

David Homer, 33, has been working in record shops since his days as a student in Norwich. However, little did he know then that his part-time job would lead to his becoming the manager of one of the biggest stores in London. David, who lives with his wife and two children, shares his story with us:

"If someone had told me years ago that I would end up with my current job, I probably would have laughed. When I was a student, I was very much against the idea of doing a nine-to-five kind of job. I didn't mind it for as long as it was on a temporary basis, but I never thought that I would turn it into a career!

It's actually hard to describe a typical day at work, as unexpected things happen all the time. The one unusual thing about working here are the hours. The store is open for 15 hours a day and, as you can imagine, we get all sorts of people coming in, not just to buy but also to look around or even escape from the cold in the street. The staff enjoy their work here, especially as they get to meet many famous singers and bands when they visit the store to present their new work.

My career does tend to be very important for me and often it comes first over other things in my life, but at least I travel back home on the train every night with a smile on my face."

London Examinations, GCE 'O' level, May 2001

49

My father and mother were nineteen that summer. They were born in 1920 and brought up in Dairy and had more or less avoided each other through the years they were growing up. It was therefore a strange coincidence that, although they had finished school without ever becoming friends, they ended up having the same summer jobs at a hotel that was, for them, so far away from home.

My mother was a waitress and served dinner and drinks dressed in her own clothes, rather than the black and white uniform that the other women who worked there used to wear. My father helped in the kitchen, carried luggage and helped the rich customers who arrived by sea get on and off their boats.

They were first introduced to each other at the staff party that took place on the first day of their arrival. Neither of them could have imagined meeting someone from back home at such a strange place! When the short party was over and everyone started getting ready for the evening's work, my father approached my mother and told her how nice it was to meet someone from Dairy, especially as they were both alone in a new place. 'We were very polite to each other, that first time, I remember that', Mother told us. 'Although we didn't know very much about each other, it was enough that we came from the same town.'

London Examinations, GCE 'O' level, January 2002

50

I finally publicly confess my love for Bessie!

She first came into my life eight years ago, on my birthday. I must admit that, although I liked her immediately, my love for her was nothing special. It was when I went to university and she came with me that we became truly inseparable. I couldn't go anywhere, not even to buy milk or the newspaper, without her. We'd go together from the library to my classes, from my classes to the cafeteria, from the cafeteria back to the library. Three years later, it's still the same. My parents, who first brought Bessie to the house all those years ago, can't believe I haven't got rid of her yet! How can I? Bessie and I have traveled miles together, seen new places, met new people, and visited friends in the middle of the night. Not once did she disappoint me! When I have to leave her out in the rain, I feel so sorry for her and apologise from the bottom of my heart! So far, she has always forgiven me.

Bessie, my bicycle, is the best birthday present I have ever had. She is beautiful, light and fast. She has soul and history. She changes colour whenever I want. She can take me from my house to the city centre in 5 minutes. Parking is always easy. She is useful in other ways too. On a bicycle you can't be lazy and as I don't do sports, Bessie provides me with all the exercise I need. She doesn't cost much and, more importantly, doesn't pollute the air.

London Examinations, GCE 'O' level, May 2002

PART TWO

51

When Greece became an independent country in 1833 the 'Katharevousa' was adopted as the official language. This form of Greek was never spoken. The Greeks always used the 'Demotic'. Adamantios Koraes is considered as the intellectual who suggested the 'Katharevousa' as the "middle solution" between the archaic form and the Demotic. John Psycharis, a Greek professor in Paris was a great supporter of the 'Demotic'. The language question divided the Greek people for many years. The 'Katharevousa' was seen as the language of the officials and the government and the 'Demotic' as the language of the ordinary people. Even those who used 'Katharevousa' at work, never used it with their families and friends – they too, spoke in the 'Demotic'. In 1976, the 'Demotic' became the official language of the state and in 1982 the 'One Accent System' was introduced by the Greek government.

Notes

independent = ανεξάρτητος, -η, -ο
adopt = καθιερώνω, υιοθετώ
official = επίσημος, -η, -ο
intellectual = ο διανοούμενος, η
language question = το γλωσσικό ζήτημα
middle solution = η μέση λύση
form = ο τύπος, είδος
ordinary = απλός, -ή, -ό
one accent system = το μονοτονικό σύστημα

supporter = υποστηρικτής, οπα-δός
I divide = διαιρώ, χωρίζω
state = το κράτος
I introduce = εισάγω

52

This is the story of a quarrel between two rich families and of how it brought grief and bloodshed to both.

It happened more than five hundred years ago in Verona, a small city in the north of Italy. The two families were called Montague and Capulet. The quarrel was so old that no-one could remember how it had begun.

The Montague family had a son named Romeo, seventeen years old, dark and handsome. The Capulet family had a daughter called Juliet. She was still very young, only just turned fourteen, but she looked older. She had gold hair and grey-green eyes and a beautiful slim body. Her parents had kept her mostly at home with an old nurse.

Romeo fell in love with Juliet during a feast given by Capulet where he attended disguised by a mask. Romeo won Juliet's consent to a secret marriage and with the help of Friar Lawrence they are wedded the next day. During a quarrel, Tybalt, from the Capulet household, kills Mercutio, a friend of Romeo whereupon Romeo kills Tybalt in revenge. The Prince orders Romeo's banishment from Verona. Romeo spends the last night with Juliet. Capulet proposes to marry Juliet to Count Paris but she seeks excuses to avoid this.

Juliet consults the friar who bids her consent to the match, but on the night before the wedding drink a potion which will render her apparently lifeless for 42 hours. He will warn Romeo, who will rescue her from the vault on her awakening and carry her to Mantua. The friar's message to Romeo miscarries, and Romeo hears that Juliet is dead. Buying poison, he comes to the vault and after a last kiss on Juliet's lips, drinks the poison and dies.

Juliet awakes and finds Romeo dead by her side and the cup still in his hand. Guessing what has happened she stabs herself and dies. The Montagues and the Capulets faced by the tragic results of their enmity are reconciled.

Notes

quarrel = ο καυγάς
grief = η θλίψη
bloodshed = η αιματοχυσία
Capulets = οι Καπουλέτοι
dark = μελαχρινός, -ή, -ό
Montagues = οι Μοντέκηδες
handsome = γενναίος, ωραίος
just turned = μόλις έκλεισε (έγινε)
slim body = λεπτό σώμα (κορμί)
nurse = η παραμάνα
disguise = η μεταμφίεση
banish = εξορίζω
feast = το γλέντι
household = το σπιτικό, αρχοντικό
propose = προτείνω, εισηγούμαι

I consult = συμβουλεύομαι
potion = μεθυστικό φάρμακο (ερωτικό φίλτρο)
rescue = γλυτώνω
miscarry = παραπέφτω
I guess = υπολογίζω, φαντάζομαι
enmity (hatred) = το μίσος
consent = η συγκατάθεση
revenge = η εκδίκηση
I avoid = αποφεύγω
friar = ο καλόγηρος, ο μοναχός
to render = παρασταίνω
vault = η νεκρική κρύπτη
poison = το δηλητήριο
I stab = μαχαιρώνω
I reconcile = συμφιλιώνω

53

They spent the rest of the afternoon shopping and got back to the hotel tired out, having booked their flight to Salonica on the morning plane. Joan said, "There is one thing I must do tonight, Joe, before leaving Athens. I must write to Nicholas and tell him what's happened."

In the warm night of the early Greek summer she sat down and wrote me a long letter. I got that letter early in June. It was a misty, dark morning with a light rain falling. In the street below the taxis went past.

It was a long letter from a very happy girl telling me about her love. She wrote of all the wonderful sights she visited and the kind-hearted people she met, and how she practised her Greek she had learned in England.

Notes

I spend = ξοδεύω, περνώ
rest = το υπόλοιπο
tired out = εξαντλημένος, -η, -ο (κουρασμένος, -η, -ο)
flight = η πτήση
misty = ομιχλώδης, -ης, -ες

dark = σκοτεινός, -ή, -ό
I book = προκρατώ
what has happened = τι συνέβηκε, τι έγινε
light rain = η ψιλή βροχούλα

54

Peter: I've been waiting twenty minutes for this bus. Do they always take so long to come?

Mary: In the morning and in the afternoon. Is this the first time you've taken it? I don't remember you from other mornings.

Peter: The first time, yes, and the last, I hope. My car broke down yesterday. If it weren't for that I wouldn't be here.

Mary: I used to take my car into town, but I gave that up a long time ago. I could never find anywhere to park, and when I did, I'd come back and find I'd been given a ticket.

Peter: Well, I've got a Mini, and parking's not so bad with a small car. Without the car I don't know what I'd do. It's so much more convenient that I think it's worth paying the fine.

Notes

take so long = αργώ, καθυστερώ
if it weren't = αν δεν ήταν
the first and the last = η πρώτη και η τελευταία φορά
I gave up = σταμάτησα, παράτησα

convenient = βολικός, -ή, -ό
ticket, fine = το πρόστιμο
broke down = χάλασε
to park = σταθμεύω, παρκάρω
not so bad = δεν είναι τόσο άσχημο

55

John: You must feel good! In a few days, your name will be up there outside the theatre. You'll be a star.

Mary: A star? I don't think of it like that. I don't really care about being famous. And anyway, you don't become famous because you work in one show. Who can promise me it's going to be a success? Nobody. There are so many unknowns in this business.

John: But this play can't fail. It's got a good author, a good director, good actors, even a good theatre. What more could you want?

Mary: You're going too fast. I don't believe in things that can't fail. In fact the one proverb I like is 'pride goes before a fall.'

Notes

I feel good = αισθάνομαι ωραία
famous = διάσημος, -η, -ο
I care = νοιάζομαι, ενδιαφέρομαι
show = η θεατρική παράσταση
to fail = αποτυγχάνω
proverb = η παροιμία
star = το αστέρι (του θεάτρου)
I promise = υπόσχομαι
pride goes before a fall = η περηφάνια προηγείται της πτώσης (αποτυχίας)

success = η επιτυχία
unknowns = άγνωστα
business = η επιχείριση (το επάγγελμα)
author = ο συγγραφέας
director = ο παραγωγός, ο σκηνοθέτης
actor = ο, η ηθοποιός

56

Most of us have a picture of a fat man as a healthy, happy, friendly person. Professor Ann James argued that this may be so but fat men are certainly not as healthy. As a general rule, the fatter you are, the shorter your life will be. A lot of nonsense has been talked about slimming and even the experts don't agree on the best diet. I myself think that it doesn't matter much if the food you eat gives you the right amount of nutrition. The quantity will depend of course, on how much exercise you get in your job. There's also an advantage in eating a little frequently rather than having two or three big meals.

Notes

picture = η εικόνα, γενική εντύπωση
rule = ο κανόνας
nonsense = η ανοησία
expert = ο, η ειδικός
nutrition = η θρέψη
nutritional = θρεπτικός, -ή, -ό
quantity = η ποσότητα
exercise = η εξάσκηση

advantage = το πλεονέκτημα, το προτέρημα
healthy = ο, η υγιής
I argue = υποστηρίζω, ισχυρίζομαι
shorter life = πιο σύντομη (μικρή) ζωή
slimming = το αδυνάτισμα
diet = η δίαιτα

57

Anne told her husband George, that they ought to have the sitting-room done up. The wallpaper was beginning to peel and the paint was scratched in some places where the children had been playing. George agreed that it looked a bit of a mess and said he would do the room up as soon as he had a weekend free. Anne said that she had not thought he would have time to do it himself. She added that he always lost his temper if things went wrong. Perhaps it would be better to leave the job to someone else. George thought she meant that he was not capable of decorating the room himself but she said that was not true.

Notes

sitting-room = το καθιστικό

wallpaper = η ταπετσαρία

to peel = ξεκολλώ
scratch = ξύνω, σχίζω
a bit of a mess = λίγο ακατάστατο
temper = θυμός, ψυχραιμία

capable = ικανός, -ή, -ό
decoration = η διακόσμηση
if things went wrong = όταν τα πράγματα πήγαν στραβά

58

The school I went to was a State school, for my father, thank God, was not a snob. He had five children to educate, and although he had an income which was considered large in those days he had plenty to do with his money – himself to keep in Egypt, and all of us in England, and the expenses of the voyages to and fro whenever leave came his way. If we went to a State school when we were young there would be more money to spare when we grew up and needed it; more important than all, we could win scholarships from a State school at an earlier age than we could win scholarships from any other school.

Notes

state school = κρατικό (δημόσιο) σχολείο
snob = σνομπ
himself to keep = για τη συντήρησή του
voyage = το ναυτικό ταξίδι
to educate = μορφώνω, σπουδάζω, εκπαιδεύω
income = το εισόδημα

scholarship = η υποτροφία
I consider = θεωρώ
whenever leave came his way = όποτε τα κατάφερνε να παίρνει άδεια
important = σπουδαίος, α, ο, σημαντικός, ή, ό
spare = διαθέσιμος, η, ο, περίσσιος, α, ο

59

Computers affect almost everyone in the modern world but most people either despise them or are afraid of them. Some think they are just enormous adding machines while others regard them as superhuman electronic brains that will eventually dominate the human species. Neither of these ideas is correct.

A computer has the power to calculate at superhuman speed and so it can quickly solve problems that would take any human mathematician years of work. It has a memory for storing information that is far more reliable than human memory. But what matters most in a computer is its programme.

Notes

computer = ο κομπιούτερ, ο υπολογιστής
affect = επηρεάζω
despise = μισώ, αντιπαθώ
dominate = κυριαρχώ, επικρατώ
human species = το ανθρώπινο είδος
memory = η μνήμη
what matters most = το κυριότερο, η πιο μεγάλη σημασία
power = η δύναμη, η ικανότητα
superhuman speed = υπεράνθρωπη ταχύτητα
adding machine = η αθροιστική μηχανή
solve = λύνω
reliable = αξιόπιστος, έγκυρος, η, ο
mathematician = ο μαθηματικός
store information = συγκρατώ, συγκεντρώνω πληροφορίες

60

The young king came to a country that was very different from his own native land. Almost eight in every ten Greeks still lived in villages, farming their small rocky, plots of land. Each family ate what they grew themselves, currants being the only product exported in any quantity. Trade on a large scale would in any case have been almost impossible for purely practical reasons. There were few roads fit for wheeled traffic even across the dusty plains; the mountain villages could be reached only by donkey or mule. To transport olive oil or wine the peasants used goatskins which were essentially not much different from those used in Homer's day.

Notes

native land = η πατρίδα
rocky = βραχώδης
grow = καλλιεργώ
currants = οι σταφίδες
product = το προϊόν
export = εξάγω
transport = μεταφέρω (η μεταφορά)

trade = το εμπόριο
large scale = μεγάλη κλίμακα
fit = κατάλληλος, η, ο
dusty = σκονισμένος, η, ο
wheeled traffic = τροχοφόρα
plain = η πεδιάδα
goatskin = το ασκί

61

In 1799 Lord Elgin was appointed British Ambassador to the Ottoman Empire. He was a lover of classical Greek art. He asked for and obtained permission from the Turkish authorities to export some of the works of art on the Acropolis. The Ottoman empire was disinterested in Greek art. In 1803 Lord Elgin began to have part of the Parthenon removed and in 1813 he transported these treasures to Britain.

Lord Byron accused Lord Elgin of being a vandal, of seeking to enrich himself at the expense of the Greeks, and of misusing his diplomatic status to accept presents from the Turks.

The quarrel between these two English peers was taken up by the English Parliament and Lord Elgin was cleared of any blame. These works of art were purchased by the government from Lord Elgin in 1816 for £35,000.

Notes

appoint = διορίζω
ambassador = ο πρεσβευτής
Ottoman empire = η Οθωμανική αυτοκρατορία
lover = ο λάτρης, εραστής
classical = κλασικός, η, ο
permission = η άδεια, συγκατάθεση
blame = η ευθύνη, ενοχή

authority = η αρχή
disinterested = αδιάφορος, η, ο
remove = αφαιρώ
treasure = ο θησαυρός
accuse = κατηγορώ
vandal = ο βάνδαλος
misuse = η κατάχρηση (καταχρώμαι)
peer = ο λόρδος

62

Early in the spring of the year 1819, when the roads were clear of snow, the organ-builder, arrived at St Nicholas Church to repair the organ.

'What did you do for music at the Christmas Mass?' he enquired, gazing thoughtfully at the sorry state of the organ.

'Oh, we managed, we managed,' answered Franz Gruber. 'Joseph Mohr, the assistant priest, wrote some verses and I set them to music. We sang them with the children at Mass and I accompanied on the guitar.'

'The guitar, eh?' exclaimed Mr Mauracher. 'I bet that caused a stir. Whoever heard of a guitar in a church?'

'Oh, it did cause a stir,' answered Franz, 'but not the kind you mean. Old Father Nostler looked down his nose a bit, of course, but most of the congregation were delighted.'

Notes

organ builder = ο διορθωτής του εκκλησιαστικού οργάνου
Mass = η λειτουργία
sorry state = θλιβερή κατάσταση
assistant = ο βοηθός
verse = ο στίχος

set to music = μελοποιώ
accompany = συνοδεύω
I bet = στοιχηματίζω
caused a stir = ξεσήκωσε κάποιο θόρυβο (θα ενόχλησε κάποιους)
congregation = το εκκλησίασμα

63

Queen Victoria was born in London in 1819. Her mother was a German princess, and her father was Edward, the fourth son of King George III.

Not many months after Victoria was born, her father died heavily in debt, leaving his family penniless. Her mother was thinking of returning to her home in Germany when her brother Prince Leopold came to her rescue and made her an allowance. The family lived on this until 1825 when Parliament recognised that Victoria was the probable heiress to the throne and voted £6,000 yearly for her education and keep.

Victoria's uncle Leopold took a great interest in her. Until he became king of the Belgians in 1831, he lived in Surrey and it was a great treat for Victoria to visit him there.

Notes

princess = η πριγκήπισσα
heavily in debt = καταχρεωμένος
penniless = απένταρος, η, ο
rescue = διασώζω, βοηθώ

allowance = το επίδομα
parliament = η βουλή
heiress = κληρονόμος, διάδοχος
keep = η συντήρηση
treat = ευχαρίστηση

64

They loved beautiful scenery. Gardens and parks and flowers were a delight to them, and they would build their monasteries on sites with the loveliest views that they could find. Beauty had an inner meaning to them. It was part of the glory of God. Life was drab and ugly; but the worshipper, the citizen in Saint Sophia or the hermit on Mount Athos was away from it all. The human architecture of the Cathedral and the divine architecture of the Mountain alike raised him out of the ordinary world and made him closer to God and True Reality. Byzantine beauty and religion went hand in hand, to their mutual advantage.

Notes

inner meaning = εσωτερικό νόημα
drab = μονότονος, άχαρος, η, ο
mutual = αμοιβαίος, α, ο
divine = θεϊκός, η, ο
advantage = το όφελος

raise = υψώνω
delight = η απόλαυση
to worship = λατρεύω, εκκλησιάζομαι
site = η τοποθεσία
hermit = ο ερημίτης

65

The Generation Gap

'Great craftsmen? Their days are over,' said Mr. S., that genius of a patisserie maker, one of the great craftsmen left in this country for whom money is nothing, quality and satisfaction of the customer is everything.

'When I retire or die,' he went on ruefully, 'that will be the end of my craft. Nobody will produce this sort of stuff; and if someone produced it people wouldn't appreciate it. They would buy and enjoy frozen muck at the supermarket. Young people are no good. I have nobody, just nobody, to pass my business and skill on to."

'I thought you had a son,' I interjected.

Mr. S. got angry.

'Yes, I do have a son. He's a good-for-nothing. A dead loss.'

I couldn't ask which prison he was in, so I put it more tactfully: 'What is he doing?'

He sighed deeply: 'He's professor of mathematics at London University.'

'How to be Decadent' by George Mikes

Notes

craftsman = ο τεχνίτης   genius = μεγαλοφυΐα, ιδιοφυΐα

patisserie-maker = ο ζαχαροπλάστης
muck = οι βρωμιές, αηδίες
appreciate = εκτιμώ
skill = η ειδικότητα
quality = η ποιότητα
rueful = θλιβερός, ή, ό

frozen = κατεψυγμένος, η, ο
satisfaction = η ικανοποίηση
retire = αποχωρώ (μπαίνω στη σύνταξη)
interject = παρεμβάλλω, παρατηρώ

66

Anyone with any pride in his intelligence ought to refuse even to sit exams, because they are an insult to both our brains and knowledge. Under the exam system you are judged on the result of a few hours' work, after having studied a subject for two years. And the examiners do not even appear to see the ludicrousness of that situation, which just shows that we who sit exams are not the only idiots the exam system produces.

If any examiner or university is really interested in whether students have anything of value to offer, then they should be marking the work that we have produced in reasonable time at school and not under the strain to remember books by heart. Exams don't prove a thing.

From a schoolgirl's letter to a British newspaper

Notes

pride = η περηφάνια
ludicrous = γελοίος, παράλογος
refuse = αρνιέμαι
insult = η προσβολή
I judge = κρίνω
idiot = ο βλάκας, ηλίθιος

situation = η κατάσταση
strain = η ένταση
knowledge = η γνώση
subject = το θέμα
value = η αξία
prove = αποδείχνω

67

Oddly enough, though so much alike, old Salamano and his dog detest each other.

Twice a day, at eleven and six, the old fellow takes his dog for a walk, and for eight years that walk has never varied. You can see them in the rue de Lyon, the dog pulling his master along as hard as he can, till finally the old chap misses a step and nearly falls. Then he beats his dog and calls it names. The dog cowers and lags behind, and it's his master's turn to drag him along. Presently the dog forges, starts tugging at the leash again, gets another hiding and more abuse. Then they halt on the pavement, the pair of them, and glare at each other; the dog with terror and the man with hatred in his eyes. Every time they're out this happens. When the dog wants to stop at a lamp-post, the old boy won't let him, and drags him on.

'The Outsider' by Albert Camus

Notes

oddly = περίεργα, παράδοξα
detest = απεχθάνομαι
vary = διαφοροποιώ
old boy = ο γεροντάκος
cower = ζαρώνω
lag = καθυστερώ, μένω πίσω

tug = τραβώ δυνατά
hiding, beating = χτυπώ
call names = βρίζω
leash = το λουρί
terror = ο τρόμος

68

And then this voice was heard from further down the bar: You want to go to Greece, old man. I would, if I were single.

Marvellous climate, bloody marvelous, four thousand years of history. Four thousand bloody years of history. They're all dying to learn English over there. They need it, you see, being a commercial nation. Anyone could go over there and get a good living. You only have to be English.' Which Kennedy indubitably was. There and then, watching the froth on his Guiness subside, he thought, why not? Scraps of myth came into his mind, culled from his haphazard but abundant reading; garlanded heifers and raped nymphs, marble columns. He would go. He would be a tutor.

"The Greeks Have a Word for It' by Barry Unsworth

Notes

single = ελεύθερος, μόνος
nation = το έθνος
You want = you should
old man = 'friend'
commercial = εμπορικός, η, ο
froth = ο αφρός
garlanded = στεφανωμένος
subside = καταλογίζω, υποχωρώ
marvelous = υπέροχος, η, ο
indubitably = αναμφίβολα
culled = picked (επιλέγω)
heifer = νεαρή αγελάδα
scrap = κομμάτι, απόσπασμα
haphazard = τυχαίος, α, ο, σκόρπιος
raped nymphs = βιασμένες νύμφες

69

'Talking of flats,' she said, 'have you heard our piece of luck? We've got a flat – at last! In Montagu Mansions.'

'Well,' said Parker, 'I've always said there are plenty of flats – at a price!'

'Yes, but this isn't at a price. It's dirt cheap. Eighty pounds a year!'

'But – but Montagu Mansions is just off Knightsbridge, isn't it? Big, handsome building. Or are you talking of a poor relation of the same name stuck in the slums somewhere?'

'No, it's the Knightsbridge one. That's what makes it so wondelful.'

'Wonderful is the word! It's a miracle. But there must be a catch somewhere. Big deposit, I suppose?'

"No deposit at all.'

'I give it up,' said Parker. 'The present occupants must be lunatics with a taste for philanthropy.'

Agatha Christie

Notes

just off = πάροδος της...
taste of philanthropy = δόση φιλανθρωπίας
dirt cheap = πάμφθηνος

deposit = η προκαταβολή
slum = η φτωχογειτονιά
catch = μειονέκτημα, παγίδα

70

English society is a class society, strictly organized. If you doubt this, listen to the weather forecasts. There is always a different weather forecast for farmers. You often hear statements like this on the radio:

'Tomorrow it will be cold, cloudy and foggy: long periods of rain will be interrupted by short periods of showers.'

And then:

'Weather forecast for farmers. It will be fair and warm, many hours of sunshine.'

You must not forget that the farmers do grand work of national importance and deserve better weather.

It happened on very many occasions that nice, warm weather had been forecast and rain and snow fell all day long, or vice versa. Some people jumped to the conclusion that something must be wrong with the weather forecasts.

George Mikes

Notes

class society = η ταξική κοινωνία
strictly organized = αυστηρά οργανωμένη
weather forecast = πρόβλεψη καιρού
doubt = αμφιβάλλω
statement = η δήλωση, ανακοίνωση
conclusion = το συμπέρασμα
grand = σπουδαίος
vice versa = το αντίθετο
interrupt = διακόπτω
showers = σύντομη πτώση βροχής
national importance = εθνική σημασία

71

For centuries they have been the backbone of trade in Britain – the traditional little corner shops and family stores in every village and town customers are greeted by name and can be assured of a friendly, personal service.

Often they are the focal point of the community. Housewives meet in them to exchange gossip while buying the groceries. Their children rush to them after school to explore the exciting wooden shelves laden with jars of sweets.

And the menfolk go there not only for their favourite brand of tobacco but because they know they will have an attentive listener as they explain their latest foolproof cure to all the world's problems.

But today the little British corner shop faces extinction.

The hard-pressed band of small, independent shopkeepers are being driven out of business in their thousands by competition from supermarkets, huge rate increases, Government restrictions and extra paperwork.

Notes

century = ο αιώνας
backbone = η βάση, η ραχοκοκαλιά
traditional = παραδοσιακός, ή, ό
greet = χαιρετώ
assure = βεβαιώνω
service = η εξυπηρέτηση
focal point = το κεντρικό σημείο
community = η κοινότητα

exchange = ανταλλάσσω
gossip = το κουτσομπολιό
shelf = το ράφι
jar = η γυάλα, το δοχείο
foolproof = αλάνθαστος, η, ο
cure = η θεραπεία
extinction = η εξαφάνιση
restriction = ο περιορισμός

72

What is taste? Good taste is not expensive says a famous interior designer and decorator. In a paper given recently to the Royal Society for the Encouragement of the Arts, he discussed at length the question of taste which, he said, affects us in every detail of life.

'It is amazing, he said, how few people bother to cultivate their taste and how very many people there are without taste, either good or bad, or any feelings about it, and all that it affects. This is only too evident when we see into the homes of our politicians, our musicians and our actors, with, of course, notable exceptions.

'It is even more obvious when we look around at what is happening to our country and to the world today. Everywhere there is total disregard for preservation and a high standard of design in manufactured goods.'

Notes

taste = το γούστο
designer = ο σχεδιαστής
decorator = ο διακοσμητής
paper (lecture) = η διάλεξη
detail = η λεπτομέρεια
cultivate = καλλιεργώ
feeling = το αίσθημα

evident = φανερό, έκδηλο
notable = αξιόλογος, η, ο
exception = η εξαίρεση
disregard = η άγνοια
manufacture = κατασκευάζω
good = το αγαθό, το εμπόρευμα

73

Gabriel Oak first meets Bathsheba Everdene when she enters his village: he falls in love with her, but is rejected. A little later, ruined by the accidental loss of his sheep, he re-encounters her as the new mistress of the farm whose hayricks he has saved from fire, and is taken on as shepherd. The rich neighbour-farmer William Boldwood, urged on by a valentine sent to him by Bathsheba, is tormented passionately for her love: but he too is rejected in favour of the dashing dragoon-sergeant Frank Troy, who wins the flattered Bathsheba as his wife. But Troy, has already had an alliance with Fanny Robin, a maidservant at Bathsheba's house: and the abandoned girl and her baby die in the Casterbridge workhouse. Troy, overcome with remorse, and with all his past life exposed, moves off, and is thought to have been drowned; but he was in fact rescued, and returns to Weatherbury as a circus-performer just when Boldwood seems certain of marrying the apparently widowed Bathsheba. In a dramatic scene Boldwood shoots Troy when he demands back his wife. Troy is killed: Boldwood is imprisoned for life as a lunatic, and the patient, devoted, dogged Oak, his rivals tragically removed, marries the sadder and wiser Bathsheba at last.

Thomas Hardy: Far from the Madding Crowd

Notes

accidental = τυχαίος, α, ο
encounter = συναντώ
dashing = εντυπωσιακός, ή, ό
flatter = κολακεύω, θέλγω
remorse = τύψεις
patient = υπομονετικός, ή, ό
rival = αντίπαλος
devoted = πιστός, αφοσιωμένος
dogged = επίμονος, ακλόνητος

reject = απορρίπτω
ruined = κατεστραμμένος, η, ο
hay-ricks = οι θημωνιές
whim = ξαφνική ιδέα
dragoon-sergeant = δραγόνος λοχίας
alliance = οι σχέσεις
workhouse = το φτωχοκομείο
apparently = φαινομενικά

74

Tess Durbeyfield is the daughter of a village huckster. When the huckster's family is in straits, Tess's sensitivity makes her think herself responsible. She therefore goes as a servant to the household of a local d'Uberville. Her father assumes the family to be akin to his own, but in reality this family is a wealthy family from the north who have taken the name before settling in Wessex as a 'country family'. Alec d'Uberville seduces Tess. She gives birth to a child which dies in infancy.

When she has recovered from the shock of these experiences Tess goes away as a milkmaid on a large farm. After many times refusing him, she becomes engaged to Angel Clare, a clergyman's son who is studying farm management at the same farm. She determines to tell him of her affair with Alec d'Uberville, but keeps putting it off, so that Angel marries her in ignorance of it. Not until their wedding night does she tell him, whereupon Angel is horrified and, after considering the situation, he abandons her and goes to Brazil. He makes some provision for her, but she is too proud to apply for any extra, which could have been obtained from his parents. Hardship comes upon her and upon her family. Her father dies, their cottage goes with him and they have nowhere to go, and, after writing pathetic and fruitless appeals to her husband, she accepts the protection of Alec d'Uberville – at the price implied.

*Thomas Hardy: Tess of the d'Uberville*s

Notes

huckster = ο ψιλικατζής, ο πραματευτής
akin = συγγενικός, η, ο
milkmaid = η αρμέχτρα
I recover = συνέρχομαι
fruitless = άγονος, η, ο
clergyman = ο κληρικός
sensitivity = η ευαισθησία
straits = η δυσχέρεια (οικονομική δυσκολία)
fruitless = μάταιος, η, ο
ignorance = η άγνοια
appeal = η έκκληση
shock = η συγκλονιστική εμπειρία
provision = οικονομική φροντίδα, η παροχή
infancy = η βρεφική ηλικία
protection = η προστασία
imply = υπονοώ, συνεπάγομαι

75

Henchard sells his wife (and little girl) to a sailor at a fair one night. Returning to his senses next morning he takes a solemn vow not to touch strong drink for twenty-one years (the age he is now). All efforts to find his wife fail.

By his energy and hard work he builds up a good corn and hay business and in time becomes Mayor of Casterbridge. Exactly eighteen years afterwards his wife returns with her daughter (supposing her sailor 'husband' to be dead). Henchard and she keep their relationship secret, and he courts her and marries her again. Henchard's business grows bigger under the capable management of a young Scot, Donald Farfrae, but Henchard quarrels with Farfrae, who sets up on his own and soon becomes a formidable rival. Mrs. Henchard dies. Henchard finds out that her daughter, whom he thought to be his (and, indeed, whom he had told that she was) is the sailor's daughter.

Farfrae rises as Henchard falls. He marries the woman Henchard expects to marry. He buys his business when he goes bankrupt and lives in his house. Henchard's degradation is complete when his past becomes known and he takes to drink once more (the twenty-one years being gone).

His step-daughter, whom he had at first treated roughly when he discovered that she was not his, in due time wins her way to his heart and turns out to be his only comfort in life, but she is now claimed by the sailor, who comes to Casterbridge to find her, and she is disgusted by the deceit of Henchard, who had concealed her parentage from her. Finally, she marries Farfrae, whose wife has died, and Henchard turns his back on the town, and comes to a wretched end in a tumbledown cottage.

Thomas Hardy: The Mayor of Casterbridge

Notes

mayor = ο δήμαρχος
solemn = σοβαρός, ή, ό
hay = το άχυρο, ο σανός
to court = ερωτοτροπώ, φλερτάρω
bankruptcy = η πτώχευση
step-daughter = θετή κόρη
tumbledown = το ετοιμόρροπο
deceit = απατηλός, ή, ό
vow = ο όρκος
corn = τα σιτηρά
formidable = φοβερός, ή, ό
rival = ο αντίπαλος
degradation = η κατάπτωση, ο ξεπεσμός
cottage = η καλύβα
roughly = σκληρά
relationship = η σχέση, ο δεσμός

76

The theme of Romeo and Juliet is a theme of love. It is a story of hatred overcome by that of love, old hate versus young love, taking no thought for the past or the future.

The atmosphere is one of passion and swiftness, full-blooded passion and rash swiftness. The whole play is in a hurry-speed into marriage, speed into banishment, speed back to Juliet, speed in another quarter to get Juliet married to Paris, speed to kill whoever steps in the way and speed to commit suicide when life suddenly seems not worth living. Romeo's haste makes him happy in his marriage, and immediately thereafter unhappy in his banishment, for had he not gone for Tybalt's blood he would never have been banished.

Notes

passion = το πάθος
banish = εξορίζω

swiftness = γρηγοράδα
banishment = εξορία

77

With 433,000 hotel beds, Greece has no shortage of accommodation. But many large island resort hotels built in the boom years of the 1970s have not been maintained to international tour operators' standards. Occupancy levels in Corfu and Rhodes have slipped in recent years.

It is no coincidence that the one era where bookings picked up sharply once the Gulf war ended was Crete, which boasts some of the best run hotels in Greece. Last year the island drew over 1.7 million tourists, close to 25 per cent of total arrivals.

Large-scale tourism didn't start in Crete till early 1980s. The resort hotels are newer and better managed and many of the mistakes made elsewhere were avoided.

Notes

shortage = η έλλειψη
occupation levels = επίπεδα κράτησης (ενοικίασης)

coincidence = η σύμπτωση
maintain = διατηρώ

78

Before the invasion the town had been an important center for tourism, with all the qualities necessary to attract foreign visitors in large quantities. Several attractive hotels overlooked its semi-circular sandy bay. The medieval castle on the cliffs to the north of the town contained the ruins of an ancient temple. The narrow streets and shady squares were filled with little shops, cafes and restaurants. From early morning until late at night the whole place was a hive of activity. Ten years later, alas, the atmosphere was very different. In the silent streets, the shutters of at least half the houses were permanently closed. Wherever you looked the buildings seemed to be crumbling away. The castle gates were locked. No wonder that the island's economy was in such a poor state!

Notes

medieval = μεσαιωνικός
shady = σκιερός, η, ο
cliff = βράχος, γκρεμός

hive of activity = πολυάσχολος χώρος

79

'How soon will you know whether the border is likely to be open today?'

The girl in the brown coat sounded irritated, but the guard merely smiled politely.

'As yet we have no instructions, madam. I have no way of telling.'

'Well, is there any way that I can telephone my London office from here?'

The guard shrugged his shoulders, somewhat less politely. 'All communications with the West are still cut. Storm damage.'

The weather had been perfect for at least two months.

The girl turned to me with a sigh. 'What use is a good story, if I can't get it through to my paper?'

I looked around cautiously, then leant forward and whispered: 'I know a way of crossing into Austria, but it'll be dangerous.'

Notes

irritated = εκνευρισμένος, η, ο

I shrugged my shoulders = σήκωσα τους ώμους αδιάφορα

80

I had been expecting a grand house with lots of windows, and a neatly kept lawn at the front. But 17 Winslow Road was one of a long street of red-brick houses, each as ordinary as the next, with no garden to speak of. Trying to relax, I rang the door-bell. At first there was no sign of life. Then I heard footsteps along the hall.

Richard, in green tee-shirt and tight-fitting blue jeans, glanced at me uncertainly. "I'm only half-awake," he apologized. "Do come in." As I stepped inside, I almost hit my head on a pale blue china bowl hanging from the ceiling. "I should have warned you about that," he said in a friendly voice. "We're all very short in my family."

Notes

lawn = το γρασίδι   uncertainly = αβέβαια

81

It is even more difficult to get a clear impression of what life was like in Greece ninety years ago than in England, for there are so many more paintings, photographs and written descriptions of life in Britain at the end of the nineteenth century. Official visitors – artists, writers, archaeologists and politicians, - have left us accounts portraying a land which was poor but full of interest. But what sort of living conditions did ordinary visitors from the West really find? Guide-books of the period advised that though it was perfectly safe to visit country areas, even for ladies, it was impossible to do without a Greek-speaking guide. Unaccompanied travellers would be obliged to carry their own beds and cook their own dinners.

Notes

painting = πίνακας, ζωγραφιά   unaccompanied = ασυνόδευτος

82

John is a tour guide. He works for one of the biggest tour operators in London, which flies in holiday visitors from the USA by the planeload, gives them a free sightseeing tour of London and then sells them other tours to places they heard about, like Oxford and Canterbury. They are escorted on these day tours by guides like John, who are paid to be informative, pleasant and amusing and, above all, not to leave anyone behind.

He enjoys working with people on holiday and his groups enjoy him, the Englishness of his accent and his sense of humour. What he doesn't enjoy are the hassles that go whith the job.

Notes

tour guide = ξεναγός   I escort = συνοδεύω

83

I traveled to South America on a cargo boat which took a whole month to reach Buenos Aires the capital of Argentina. Before I set sail I was sure I had in me more of the pioneering spirit than even Columbus himself, but I soon decided that riding the waves was not one of my strong points, for the smell of the engines in our small ship and the constant vibration turned my stomach, and I experienced none of the joys of the cruel sea. In fact I was horribly ill for almost the entire journey, although I was just able to emerge at the end of it to enjoy the unbelievable beauties of Rio, in Brazil.

Notes

cargo boat = φορτηγό πλοίο   constant = επίμονος, συνεχής

84

As king Otho left to exile, he found some consolation in the thought that the land he had come to love so much had made remarkable progress in the thirty years of his reign. Of course, to a foreign visitor, Greece still appeared a backward little kingdom, where conditions remained primitive by European standards. But its progress could only be properly measured by contrasting the present with what Otho had found when he came to Greece as a young man of seventeen. The king could not, however, take credit for all the advances. Much of the country's progress resulted from the efforts of enterprising Greeks who had amassed fortunes abroad. And in spite of such improvements the country remained largely a land of poor peasants.

Notes

consolation = παρηγοριά   enterprising = επιχειρηματικός,
reign = η βασιλεία   τολμηρός
primitive = πρωτόγονος

85

Early every morning she was woken by the noise of the traffic. The first time it happened, she got out of bed, crossed the room and opened the shutters. But the smell of petrol was so strong that she quickly closed them again. She was shocked to find the streets of Athens so noisy and so polluted. Twenty years previously things had been very different. There had been no forest of television aerials on the city rooftops in those days! She wondered whether her little whitewashed house with the flower pots on the balcony and the blue front door was still there, in a back-street of Kolonaki. It had probably been knocked down to make way for a block of flats.

Notes

pollution = η μόλυνση   shutters = τα παραθυρόφυλλα

86

What sort of food are we likely to be eating in the 21st century? Most people, when you ask them a question like that, either say: "There won't be any left," or, "Whatever it is, there won't be much taste in it." Of course there are good reasons for being pessimistic about the world's food supplies in the future. Nevertheless, not all the experts share the general despondency.

For one thing, although the world's population is rising fast, food production is keeping pace with it, even in developing countries. The main reason why people are hungry is because the food is not fairly distributed. The United Nations and the rich countries can solve the problem by giving more food and help to the poorer countries.

Notes

despondency = απόγνωση, keep pace = συμβαδίζω
μελαγχολία

87

Is there any truth in astrology? There has certainly been a growing interest in Britain over the last twenty years. More than half the population admit to glancing at the daily forecasts for their sign of the zodiac in the popular newspapers. In the same way, books explaining the subject in simple terms enjoy sales of over a million. There are plenty of amateur astrologers. When a friend of mine joined a local weekly paper, the first job given him was to write the "What the Stars Foretell."

"If you believe in the stars then you can believe in anything," said my friend. What is amazing is that in a certain newspaper one astrologer said exactly the same things about four different signs of the zodiac during the same week!

Notes

forecast = η πρόβλεψη   amateur = ερασιτέχνης

88

I looked at the photograph again. My father was grinning mischievously at the camera. He was wearing extremely baggy light-coloured trousers, trainers and a plain shirt open at the neck. Stephen was dressed similarly. They could have come from any period. Apart from the fact that it was in colour, it could have been a picture from the Thirties as easily as the Eighties. There was something incredibly alive about my father. He looked young and carefree – not like a husband with a small child. I could almost hear his laugh. It was a sunny day in the photo, just like today.

'Paul was twenty-nine when that was taken,' Stephen told me. 'I was twenty-two.'

'May I keep it?' I asked.

Notes

grin = μορφασμός
mischievously = κακόβουλα, πονηρά

carefree = ξέγνοιαστα, ανέμελα

89

No-one doubts that violence in on the increase. There have been various explanations for this. Some people have blamed the poor economic state of the country; others think that the decline in religious belief has automatically led to lower standards of morality. Television and the cinema have also been held responsible, because they present violence in a heroic light. It could be argued, however, that robbery and murder were just as common a hundred and fifty years ago, when the economy was in good shape, churches were full every Sunday and the camera had not even been invented. But we would certainly be justified in wondering why more men are guilty of violent crimes than women. Are the reasons biological, or is society to blame?

Notes

state = η κατάσταση
morality = η ηθικότητα

decline = η πτώση, παρακμή
justify = δικαιολογώ

90

Mary and Kenneth are divorcing, having been married for nine years. They have two young children, who will be living with Mary, their mother. They have always lived in rented accommodation in a small town and neither of them has any substantial capital or savings.

Kenneth's wealthy aunt died shortly after he and Mary separated. Kenneth went to his aunt's funeral but his wife did not. Under the terms of his aunt's will Kenneth has been left £100,000, which he will receive in the near future. Mary's solicitors are advising her to claim some of that money because the will was made when they were living together as husband and wife.

Notes

divorce = το διαζύγιο, χωρίζω   will = η διαθήκη
capital = κεφάλαιο

91

In a recent American case, a little girl, adopted as a baby was taken away at the age of two and a half from the only parents she had ever really known. Sobbing for her "mummy", she was strapped into a child's seat in her natural father's car and driven off. That father was a stranger so far as the child was concerned, but his rights were allowed to predominate.

TV cameras recorded the child's distress and bewilderment. Her mother, when agreeing to the adoption, had lied about the identity of the father. That resulted in a legal situation where the father's "rights" were the most important consideration, whatever the resultant trauma to a toddler might be.

Notes

I adopt = υιοθετώ
predominate = υπερισχύω

bewilderment = ταραχή, σύγχυση
I sob = κλαίω (με αναφυλλητά)

92

Adrian appeared at the kitchen door wearing a pair of tracksuit bottoms. He jumped back in surprise when he saw John. 'Why are you up so early?' he said, accusingly.

'I always get up this time,' John said. "You're the one who's up early.'

'I set my alarm. I was going to bring you breakfast in bed. I was going to run round to the newsagents and get you a paper while the kettle was boiling.'

John laughed.

'You've spoiled it now.' Adrian scratched his chest and yawned. 'Is that tea still hot?'

'What were you going to make me for breakfast?'

Adrian sat down at the table and reached for the milk carton. 'I'm not telling you,' he said, disagreeably.

Notes

accusingly = κατηγορηματικά
to yawn = χασμουριέμαι

93

Man From the Palace was an interesting book. On the face of it, it told the story of a contemporary prince who, in the first chapter, succeeds to the throne of a mythical European country: Rurimania. To discover an answer to student riots, violent crime, strikes, traffic congestion and many other problems of Western urban life, he buys a computer. The ironic humour of the book emerged as the computer gave logical, rational answers which revealed most of the Cabinet's decisions as a dogmatic nonsense. The computer was not programmed to allow for personal or national pride, and the solutions it proposed did not take into account Rurimania's history or its mistaken belief that it remained one of the big three nations of the present-day world.

Notes

contemporary = σύγχρονος   congestion = συνωστισμός
riot = ταραχή

94

The origins of Albania, Bulgaria, Romania and Yugoslavia and the establishment of their frontiers do not go far back in time. For the previous five hundred years there had been a period of empire building characterized by the extension of power of the Ottoman empire across the Danube.

Twice, in 1529 and 1683, the Ottoman advance had been halted before Vienna by the united efforts of the peoples of central Europe. After that, the Austrian rulers and the sultan of Turkey shared possession of the Balkan peninsula with frontiers that changed from time to time. The recent changes in former Yugoslavia and the tragic events in Bosnia were the result of rising nationalism.

Notes

Danube = ο Δούναβης   Ottoman = Οθωμανικός, ή, ό
peninsula = η χερσόνησος

95

Cadmus was a prince of Tyre. Zeus had fallen in love with Cadmus's sister, Europa. He had changed himself into a bull and had carried the girl away to the fields of Crete. But her father, Agenor, with no idea of what had happened, ordered Cadmus to look for the lost girl throughout the world, and gave him the punishment of exile, if he failed to find her.

So Cadmus wandered all over the world and became an exile, keeping away from his own country where his father's anger would await him. Finally, he visited the oracle at Delphi who told him to forget about his sister Europa and instead to find a cow marked with a moon-shaped sign. He should follow the cow and build a city at the first place where she should choose to lie down and rest. He followed the oracle's instructions and Cadmus built the city of Thebes.

Notes

I wander = περιπλανιέμαι   sign = σημάδι
oracle = το μαντείο

96

As I approached the post-box, I saw Matthew cycling towards me. I hadn't seen him since we left school seven months earlier, but already he had changed. He looked straight at me without surprise and got off his bicycle.

"Hello, Anna," he said. "I was wondering whether I'd run into you."

"Hi," I said, "how's things?'

We stood about a yard apart, not speaking. He was wearing smart but casual clothes, and looked awkward in them. Slightly shorter than me, with curly hair, large grey eyes and sticking-our ears, he was strangely attractive in an unusual way.

"Where are you off to?" he asked.

"Home," I said. "To walk the dog."
"Can I come along?" he asked. "I'm at a bit of a loose end right now."

Notes

to be at loose end = δεν έχω με τι να ασχοληθώ

97

When you visit Paris, don't expect life in this most beautiful of cities to mirror that of London, or assume that its people will behave like the English. Although we are all Europeans nowadays, and the Channel Tunnel has made the exchange of ideas and fashions even easier than before, many French people are still too proud of their national culture to tolerate any criticism of it. Of course, as Paris can be very romantic, most visitors will simply fall in love with the atmosphere of the place. Both the people and the architecture will amaze you with their grace and beauty. But many locals, uneasy about the changes which mass tourism has brought with it, can be quite suspicious of foreigners.

Notes

I assume = υποθέτω   grace = η χάρη
tolerate = ανέχομαι   uneasy = ανήσυχος

98

Europeans have a lot in common but it is their differences, not their similarities, which attract the attention of sociologists. 35% of Germans live alone; but only 9% of Spaniards. The British attend more adult evening classes than anyone else in Europe. The English "pub" is the place where most British people frequent for a drink and is the equivalent of the Greek "taverna".

More couples divorce in Britain every year than they do in Greece. The British think that black cats are lucky. Every other European country regards them as unlucky. The French are the most athletic Europeans. Dutch husbands do the household shopping a lot more often than Italians. Everywhere in Europe drive on the right-hand side of the road but in Britain they drive on the left. All Europeans use kilos and kilometers the British still use pounds and miles.

Notes

In common = κοινά (από κοινού)
sociologist = ο κοινωνιολόγος
frequent = συχνάζω

99

Finland is a republic with a population of about six million. The climate is severe in winter and lasts about six months. Finland's capital, Helsinki, is a small city with a population of only 500,000. Open to the sea on three sides, it is also Finland's rainest city. Its economy is based on the country's main industries: paper, shipping, metal, agriculture and tourism. Many of the places of interest in the city are within walking distance. The area around the Senate Square was built in the 19th century and has many beautiful buildings.

Finland's neighbouring countries are Russia, Norway and Sweden. Finland was conquered by Russia in 1809 and became independent after the Russian revolution of 1917.

Notes

based = βασίζεται
conquered = κυριεύτηκε

100

Saturday was a good day, the best since the foggy afternoon in the park when I had met Mark for the first time. That had been bitter February weather; it was now almost April, and the air was warm and spring-like. Mark borrowed his parents' car and drove us to a remote, rocky beach, which we had to ourselves. I sat on a rock and watched the rough sea glittering in the sun – a beach is the only place I know where I can sit and do nothing for hours on end. Mark, deciding it was warm enough to sunbathe, took off most of his clothes, lay down on a stretch of sand out of the wind, and promptly fell asleep.

Notes

bitter = τσουχτερός   remote = απόμερος, η, ο

101

Everyone agrees that misbehaviour in schools is a growing problem. What nobody can decide is who is to blame. Is it teachers, for not providing sufficiently interesting lessons? Or are the parents at fault, for not bringing up their children with a respect for authority? The explanation is almost certainly more complicated than that. Many different factors are at work. A recent study suggests, for example, that television has significantly reduced children's ability to pay attention for extended periods of time. As a result, they easily become bored. A half-hour history lesson is now too long to hold the interest of a child who is used to watching programmes which are interrupted every twelve minutes by advertisements.

Notes

misbehaviour = κακή συμπεριφορά   authority = η εξουσία
factor = παράγοντας

102

When I was an undergraduate in London, I travelled twice a day for seven stops on the Circle Line of the underground railway, and that became a most useful, regular time for reading, of which I had a great deal to do at that period. I learned to read standing on the escalator, getting on and off the trains, waiting on the platforms, and I developed a kind of inner timebell which sounded when we had arrived at Temple Station.

We once had a hideously cramped, hot, slow train journey to Italy and 'Martin Chuzzlewit' saw my husband happily through most of it. Journeys are obvious occasions for reading. Journeys on trains go best with very long, realistic novels, or really first-class thrillers, and the scenery had better be dull. Journeys by air, unless you are much calmer than me, cannot be enjoyed but only endured, and I'm not sure that any book can supply exactly what I need, which is to be uplifted, diverted and tranquillised simultaneously. Reading in cars is mostly impossible. It makes you sick.

But then, much travelling time is not spent in travelling, at all, but in waiting, and it is in all the waiting rooms of life that we need books more than anywhere else.

EXAMINATION PAPERS

103

As he made his way down the dark staircase, he could already feel the insistent beat of the music in the air. Inside the packed room the noise was truly deafening. He stood for a moment in the doorway, trying to spot Jason in the crowd, but the sweating dancers all looked the same under the flickering lights. Pushing his way to the bar, he ordered a mineral water. The glass was pleasantly cold. But before he had time to take a sip, he felt a hand on his shoulder. "I thought you were never going to turn up", said a familiar voice. "Fancy a stroll outside? If I stay in here much longer, I shall faint from the heat."

London Examinations, GCE 'A' level, May 1998

104

Even in Britain it is surprisingly easy to arouse public interest in the destruction of South American rain forests, or to persuade people to contribute to a fund for the victims of an Asian earthquake. It would be much harder to find a team of volunteers prepared to clear the rubbish from a village stream or repair a stone wall. Such jobs are neither exciting nor exotic. Yet, it is to tackle tasks of this sort that the new group Environment For All has been formed. Yesterday they held their first press conference in a London park. "Let us forget about endangered species and the effects of the hole in the ozone layer", said a spokesperson. "It is time to clear up the mess on our own back doorstep."

London Examinations, GCE 'A' level, May 1998

105

As he waited for the bus outside the factory gate, he began to look around nervously. He was not familiar with this part of the town, which had a bad reputation. There was hardly anyone around, apart from a group of three or four teenagers leaning against the grimy shutters of a greengrocer's shop. They all had short haircuts and large boots. Without meaning to, he found himself staring at them and looked hurriedly away. There was no sign of a bus. He wondered whether it would be wiser to telephone for a taxi. Suddenly he felt a tap on his arm. As he swung round, one of the gang thrust a tattered piece of paper at him. "You're Chinese, aren't you? said the youth. "What does this say?"

London Examinations, GCE 'A' level, May 1999

106

Their representative has strong views about public transport. In his opinion, if leading politicians are suddenly anxious to persuade more people to use public transport, the reason for this change in policy is not difficult to find. "Cars," he said in a recent speech, "are bad for the environment. The more roads you build, the more cars use them. Town centres are being turned into gigantic car-parks. But what are the alternatives? Have you tried travelling by train recently? Having paid a small fortune for your ticket you will be lucky if it arrives at all. Perhaps the government should simply pay us to stay at home."

London Examinations, GCE 'A' level, May 1999

107

"How did you get here so quickly", asked Peter. "I thought you were coming by train. I wasn't expecting you for another hour at least." He seemed rather annoyed. Ann put her suitcase down and closed the front-door gently behind her. Catching sight of her reflection in the hall mirror, she instinctively checked to see that her hair was tidy.

"When I rang the station to ask about train times, I discovered that I couldn't get here before half past five, so I drove down. Conditions were good nearly all the way. The traffic is relatively light at this time of day, although there were several lorries in front of me when I joined the motorway. I even had time to stop for a cup of coffee".

London Examinations, GCE 'A' level, May 2000

108

Though they are reluctant to acknowledge it, the British have a problem with old age. As the number of elderly people increases, the facilities for caring for them are becoming overstretched. In Mediterranean countries, the younger members of a family take it for granted that they will look after their parents, and even aunts and uncles, when they are too frail to care for themselves. Here there is no such expectation. Traditionally, British sons and daughters leave home at a younger age and lead more independent lives than do their southern counterparts. As a result, the bonds between family members are often much weaker than in Greece or Italy. Consequently, what once would have been seen as a natural duty is now sometimes regarded as an unreasonable burden.

London Examinations, GCE 'A' level, May 2000

109

Julian Lloyd Webber, the successful composer, expressed his fears about the future of classical music, in a recent interview. Two years ago, he asked the big television channels to give daily three-minute slots to young classical artists for a week. "Surprisingly, they accepted. But they didn't follow it up!" he says. "It's a battle to make classical music be heard by more people. The media don't help either. There are hardly any music reviews in the press and some composers even feel that if their music is played in a popular radio station and people like it, there must be something wrong with it!"

Lloyd Webber isn't afraid of appearing at big events, so he's playing at an open-air concert in Hyde Park, next month. "It's part of reaching a wider public. Last year, there were nearly 40,000 people in the concert in the park!"

EDEXCEL, GCE 'A' level, June 2001

110

Over the years, respect for the environment has come to take on a similar meaning for most of us; we no longer throw away bottles, newspapers and magazines. Instead, at the end of the week we make the trip to the special containers that the city council has placed in various areas and deposit the items that can be recycled. We smile to the like minded people who are doing the same thing and then off we go, pleased with ourselves. However, how many of us would sacrifice a Sunday in order to help clean a beach or plant trees?

There are those who claim that, in order to do something more effective for the environment, recycling is simply not enough. What we need is to educate our young into recognising the importance of a safe and healthy environment and realising that its protection is everyone's responsibility.

EDEXCEL, GCE 'A' level, June 2002

111

Studies have long proved that a healthy person, who does not smoke, exercises regularly, takes particular care of his diet and avoids alcohol, tends to be happier, is less likely to fall ill and lives longer. Worried that your life style doesn't really allow you to practice all, or even some, of the above? Do not despair! Here's the latest from research done at the University of Kansas in the U.S.A. Results from studies carried out by the medical department there have indicated that giving blood at least three times a year not only gives you the opportunity to have a free medical check but also reduces by almost 50% the possibility of suffering from a heart condition or contracting a serious illness!

EDEXCEL, GCE 'A' level, June 2003

112

On June 26, Nantucket was placed on the list of the 11 most threatened historic places in the country, according to the National Society for the Preservation of Buildings. The situation is particularly severe on this small island off the coast of Massachusetts because the development of tourism over the last few years has been responsible for the destruction of some of the most important historic buildings. The fact, however, that Nantucket is now on the list means that people will become more aware of the threat from development plans that are not sensitive to the traditional architecture of the area.

The National Society claims that Nantucket's historic character, the attraction that draws visitors to the island, is in danger of disappearing completely if they continue to tear down the old buildings instead of repairing them.

EDEXCEL, GCE Advanced Unit 2 - 2004

113

A Greek minister asks for the return of the Elgin marbles. Mr Venizelos in his letter to the director and curators of the British Museum states that: "In order to reinforce the clear cut position on the return of the Parthenon marbles to Greece, I have to repeat one more time that the Greek government has never acknowledged that the Parthenon Marbles belong legally to the British Museum. The position of the Greek government is that it does not discuss the legal issues because it wishes to find a solution acceptable to both sides, which would allow the marbles to be exhibited as whole in the new Acropolis Museum".

EDEXCEL, GCE Advanced Unit 2 - 2003

114

On the one hand there were the tightly knit, mutually supportive communities in the old villages of England. On the other there is the awful spectacle of youths wandering aimlessly through our decaying city centres, the absurd nationalism that tore Europe apart in the 20th century and the terrorism of the 21st.

We in these islands have much of which to be proud. We have a tolerant society with a long record of accepting into our country immigrants from every corner of the world. Naturally enough, as in all societies, we British are more comfortable in the company of those whose social values and attitudes we share. In fact there is less prejudice on the grounds of race in England than in most of the rest of the world. I believe that our problems are cultural not racial.

EDEXCEL, GCE Advanced Unit 2 - 2006

115

On 23 March 2005 the European Union adopted an initiative for youth in Europe. This initiative is aimed at improving training and job opportunities for young people. Thus it will be possible for them to live and work in other EU countries.

The goal is to help a generation of young Europeans to integrate well into work and social life. The initiative also seeks to introduce measures to prevent failure at school. Employers and businesses will be asked to employ more young people. The measures will encourage them to be more ambitious. Furthermore it will be possible for young Europeans to study in other EU countries.

Knowledge of other languages and cultures is becoming even more important in Europe today.

EDEXCEL, GCE Advanced Unit 2 - 2007

116

Millions of people around the world depend on financial support from wealthy governments and other charity organisations. These organisations will provide them with the basic necessities, such as clean water, schoolbooks and food. In the best cases this assistance helps communities become more independent. In this way, in the future, they will not need to rely on what others offer them.

Here is an example of how the international community can offer positive help to a developing country. Education in Tanzania was private until recently, so many children could not go to school. In January the government offered free primary education and hundreds of children sat at desks for the first time in their lives. The children in Tanzania want to learn but there are not enough buildings or books.

EDEXCEL, GCE Advanced Unit 2 - 2008

117

Not many people know that Cyprus has a rich film history. Since 1960, many films have been made by Cypriot directors or in Cyprus. Perhaps the most well known Cypriot director is Michael Cacoyiannis, famous for his 1964 film "Zorba the Greek".

In 2006, the Cyprus International Film Festival was created to invite new artists to show their talent and compete for the first prize. Recently, the government has given the green light for a committee to look at ways to encourage foreigners to make films in Cyprus.

With mountains, sea and cities, Cyprus could be the perfect destination for local and foreign directors!

EDEXCEL, GCE Advanced Unit 2 - 2010

118

I am not on Facebook and I do not intend to be, ever! I simply do not see the point! Most of the people there, who would know me either from school or university or work, would not bother to contact me in the real world. Why should it be different on the Internet?

Why would I want to communicate with people who have not called me or written to me in ten years, just because they happen to be in my list of "friends" on a website? My real friends have my number and address and know where to find me. Besides, I often hear complaints from people who are members, that they feel unloved if no ones sends them a message or writes on their wall for a day or two!

EDEXCEL, GCE Advanced Unit 2 – 2011

119

Many environmental problems nowadays are caused by things people do on a day-to-day basis. We waste energy at home by leaving the lights on. We use our cars more than necessary. We throw away food. We buy things we do not need.

Here is some advice about simple things we can do to be more environmentally friendly. Buy food which is fresh and in season. This means that we waste less energy transporting and refrigerating it. Reuse or recycle, instead of throwing things away. This saves money and energy.

EDEXCEL, GCE Advanced Unit 2 – 2012

120

A new documentary series examines the relationship between television characters and society over the past six decades. The fashion and clothes may change but the stereotypes remain.

We have seen thousands of characters on television since it started. "The independent woman", "the honest policeman", "the handsome doctor", "the funny family man", "the young couple", "the brave soldier", are just some of the classic roles we see. However, there are just four categories, which, in fact, made their first appearance in ancient Greek literature.

EDEXCEL, GCE Advanced Unit 2 – 2013

121

Many people are able to speak two languages fluently or maybe three or even four. However, Ioannis Ikonomou is comfortable speaking thirty or so.

In a telephone interview with a Greek newspaper from his office in Belgium , the translator says he began learning English, his first foreign language, at the age of six.

"I liked it so much, nothing could stop me", says Ikonomou, whose mother tongue is Greek.

When he learns a new language, Ikonomou says he lives and breathes everything connected to it. He spends time studying the language, of course, but also the people, who speak it and the food they eat.

EDEXCEL, GCE Advanced Unit 2 – 2014